The Teenager's Guide to Becoming a Professional Soccer Player

D1605623

James Weber

This book is dedicated to the dreamers.

Table of Contents

Introduction

Congratulations! You have taken the first step towards your dreams by opening this book and finding out the secrets to becoming a professional soccer player. This book will expand your knowledge and teach you how to better yourself for accomplishing everything you put your mind to. Through out this book, you will learn advice on mental, physical, tactical, and emotional aspects of life and the game of soccer itself. Take every bit of advice and put it into place in your life. Be ready to take action after reading this book and never look back. Your dreams are ready to be conquered and this book is that first step necessary to hit the ground running.

As a professional soccer player himself, the author of this book, James Weber, passes on the pieces of advice that he has learned through out his career. Now, as Weber shares that advice with you, he helps give you an inside look on how he learned that advice by providing personal stories after every tip. There are a hundred pieces of advice in this guide, and you can't just follow a few of them and expect to be prosperous. You need to take it all in and keep it in your heart. Professional soccer players don't achieve greatness by taking their dreams lightly. They are constantly giving 100% of their effort and fighting for more from life and from the game of soccer.

While reading this book, if you ever feel intimidated or that this all may be too much for you, remember how great your life will be when you are making hundreds of thousands or even millions of dollars doing what you love. Nothing can stop you. Dedicate yourself to the game and keep this book with you at all times as a reminder that anything is possible. Weber accomplished his dreams and he didn't have access to this advice or a book like this at an early age. Now, as a veteran professional soccer player in Europe, he is giving you the head start that you need to one day be in his shoes. Dream big. Have faith. And let every piece of advice through out this book help boost you towards achieving your dreams of one day playing professional soccer.

1. Stay Focused.

Setting goals is never easy. Picking careers is even harder. But if playing professional soccer is truly what you want to do, then understand that the path there is far from easy. There will be obstacles and distractions, but if your focus remains on point, then it will remain possible.

Focus doesn't just pertain to life on the soccer field. Focus needs to be a 24/7 thing. Your focus on your dreams is the first step to achieving them. As a soccer player, you spend most of your time off of the field, but you need to spend that time focusing on your performance and improvement on the field. The amount of distractions is always growing, especially through out high school and into college. You will have people doubting you and telling you to choose a different career, but this "white noise," as I call it, has no place in the mind of a dreamer.

Focus is constantly being challenged, and most of the time, that challenge is in the form of doubt. That doubt usually is coming from one's self. Soccer careers are filled with ups and downs from the age of 4 until 50 and even beyond at times. The only time doubt should come before focus is in the dictionary. Set a goal of becoming a professional soccer player and stay committed until that dream becomes a reality. Then, dream even bigger.

Story: I have wanted to be a professional soccer player since I was 8-years-old. People always tried to tell me that I needed to find a "real" career, or a goal that was actually attainable. They laughed at me, and to be honest I laughed back as I knew that they did not understand. I laughed because I knew something they didn't know: my focus is unbreakable. And yours should be the same.

2. Create a Vision Board.

A vision board is a display of what you want your future to look like. One way to create a vision board is to cut out positive quotes or pictures of your dream cars, houses, players, teams, or goals from magazines, or you can just print pictures off the Internet and glue them onto a poster board. This is a way that you can put all of your greatest dreams and goals together on one canvas. Now, put that board somewhere in your bedroom where you will see it every single day. Use this as a daily reminder of your dreams, so your focus can never fade.

On your vision board, put a picture of your favorite soccer player. Put up a jersey of your favorite professional team with your last name on it. Put your dream house that your first professional contract is going to buy you, or that Lamborghini that you will be driving through the city to practice every day at the stadium. Once you have created this vision board, spend a few minutes or even seconds reassuring yourself that these pictures aren't just dreams, but rather they are your future. Reassure yourself that you will do whatever it takes until your vision board becomes your reality. Your reality is in your hands, or I should say, "at your feet."

Story: I hadn't learned about vision boards until recently when my wife told me about the idea. I thought it was stupid at first, but then I made one and my motivation was pushed beyond any point it had been at before. Physically seeing my dreams in front of me gave me a drive that was overwhelming. And I have already gone through a couple vision boards, as I just keep achieving what I had pictured on them. Don't underestimate the power of a vision board. Give it a shot, trust me.

3. Surround yourself with positivity.

As a big dreamer, it is hard to find people who are as dedicated as you are. Chances are, you won't find anyone with your drive and passion for the sport. However, you can always find people who don't second-guess your passion, and who pour even more fuel into your fire towards chasing your dreams. Of course, these positive people are hard to find. But once you find one, keep him or her close. And try to reciprocate the positivity. We are subconsciously a mirror of the people we surround ourselves with, so be careful when choosing them.

As teenagers, you will come across many negative influences that will try and drag you down with them into a hole that is hard to get out of. Push those people away, and you will soon get better at determining who will pull you up and who will drag you down. This type of ability will be very helpful in your future. Find friends who motivate you and understand your goals. You may not always be the most popular, and you may not have the most friends in school, but your future will be brighter than any "popular" partier.

Story: I had gotten into the "cool" crowd in high school. I was invited to parties and had lunch with all of the jocks. Then I got offered a beer at one of the first parties I went to. I took a step back as I analyzed my whole life. I turned down the beer, called my dad to come pick me up, and never hung out with those friends again. In fact, I dropped everyone and socially started over. If I hadn't, my soccer career may have ended before I even got out of high school. That was one of the best choices I ever made. Stay out of trouble and surround yourself with positivity.

4. Set daily goals.

At the beginning of every week, break down each day within it. Create a clear plan with your improvement in mind. Write down your daily routine and stick to it. Write down your diet plan, your practice plan, and any other social duties. Make achievable goals when it comes to carb in-take, practice hours, or pages in a book you are reading. Setting goals makes us conscious of our tasks at hand, and it reassures that we won't forget about them. Taking the time every morning to break down a day will make things less chaotic and refresh our minds. We will become so aware of our daily improvements that over time, we will seek improvement constantly, without writing any plans down. Setting goals, whether it's the amount of touches on a ball or the number of push-ups we do in a row, will ultimately make us goal-driven, and therefore fearless of the size of our goals.

If you find this type of exact goal-setting hard, try writing down at least 5 ways how you are going to improve each day, whether as a soccer player, a student, or a person. This adjustment will again make you aware of your own abilities, and create life habits that lead to your constant seeking of self-improvement.

Story: As a professional soccer player, I was daily writing goals for myself pertaining to how many juggles I got or the number of hours I spent in the gym. Over time, I noticed that my goals were not just becoming easier to achieve, but that my daily goal setting went beyond my morning routine. I would walk into a room and create a goal for myself. Maybe it was, "introduce myself to 5 new people" or "discover at least 5 mistakes made in the soccer game that was on the television." I noticed that I was constantly setting goals for myself, and always seeking my own improvement. This all started simply by just writing down my daily goals in a journal.

5. Regret nothing.

We all make mistakes. We all end up on the wrong side of a decision or on the losing side of a competition. We all get injured or miss a crucial shot. I have realized one thing from all of these downfalls through out my career: Forget it! If you forget about all of the bad things, you have nothing to regret. Therefore, you become happier and less worrisome. If you dwell on the past, you are just wasting time. So what - you missed a breakaway? So what - you scored an own goal? It happens to the best of us. We can't take time away from focusing on our goals. Regret leads to time that we can never get back. So, look forward, forget the negatives, and chase your dreams.

If you are having a hard time with this, then get back out on the soccer field. The best way to forget a loss is to do what you love. Put a ball back at your feet and improve your skills. When you make a mistake, make your next move worth remembering, so everyone forgets about when you lost the ball. That translates to life as well. In any aspect, people will only be reminded of your downfalls if you let it affect your future performance. The sooner you forget about the negatives, the quicker you can move on to creating positives.

Story: I used to be the worst at dwelling on the past. I would miss a breakaway in the 2nd minute of a game and it would stick with me until the final whistle blew. It wasn't until I was 20 or so that I realized I needed to stop my whining, stop my regretting, and just move on. Now, whenever I mess up, I take a deep breath. Then, I chase back and get open to receive the ball as soon as possible. When I get the ball, I complete a simple pass and I congratulate myself. Even if it is a little 6-yard open pass, I use it to create momentum for myself for the rest of the game. Starting at that moment, I am 1 for 1 in completed passes and I know I will go 1 for 1 on my next shot on goal.

6. Take no days off.

If you truly want to become a professional soccer player, every day must be taken full advantage of. We have to treat life like we are on borrowed time, and not waste a single second. Every second is an opportunity for us to improve and advance our career. Even when you are injured, or the day after a rough game, you can still turn on a soccer match on TV and study the players in your position. You can watch film of yourself, or get in an upper-body workout. If you think about taking a day off to rest and lay in bed, just remember that your competitors are probably out improving themselves. Being talented isn't always in your hands, but being a hard worker is.

Get in the habit of always having something planned. Never leave a day open or lacking self-improvement. Laying around causes atrophy in your muscles and will weaken your motivation. Never be that person that is comfortable with just being comfortable. Pushing yourself to your limits is a better habit than lying around and eating potato chips.

Story: The first time I had knee surgery, I spent the first couple weeks of recovery lying around and just feeling sorry for myself. Then, one day, I was scrolling through Facebook and I saw a video of one of my high school rivals training. This made me sick to my stomach. He was out working his ass off to get better and here I was getting fat on the couch, drowning in my sorrows. "No more," I thought to myself. I scheduled more physical therapy sessions and I wrote out a daily plan minute-by-minute on how I could improve as a soccer player even though I was incapable of running. I studied games. I did abdominal workouts. I trained with reflex exercises. I wasn't going to take any more days off. I was going to fight.

7. Love yourself.

Especially as teenagers, we are constantly shown images of people we wish we could be. We get this image in our minds that we should look a certain way or play a certain way. We are told that we need to be like this or that. I think it's all crap. Love who you are and embrace it. The second you start fading away from who you truly are is the second you will start fading away from the sport you love and the dreams you put in place for yourself. Never be scared of staying true. Not everyone will like you, and barely anyone will think you are perfect. But as long as you know you are amazing, talented, and that your future is bright, the rest of the voices are irrelevant.

Everyone struggles to love him or herself at one point or another. We all face scrutiny and this causes our self-perception to be challenged. We can't let people change how we think, because that type of weakness will allow people to change who we are. Think of yourself as a future professional soccer player, and love that person. No one should sway your thoughts, and definitely no one should sway your feelings.

Story: When I was in high school, I was made fun of because I didn't drink or party. I started to hate who I had become, even though I was doing exactly what I should have been doing. If I would have let everyone's opinions affect my own opinion of myself, I would have been depressed. But then I would score a hat trick and beat our cross-town rivals and I would think to myself, "I love who I am. I love where I'm going. And there is nothing you guys can do about it." Have that attitude, and you will go far in life.

8. Touch a ball daily.

You don't want to be that player that receives a hard pass and your first touch flies 10 yards away from you. There is an easy way to avoid this: live with a ball at your feet. Make it a goal to touch a soccer ball at least once a day. Getting used to having a ball at your feet daily will improve your ability when you are on the field running full speed and need to control a ball. Sometimes, the best practice is just dribbling up and down the field, getting as many touches as possible on the ball. Our bodies and our muscle memory go a long way for us soccer players. The more we touch a soccer ball, the more natural it comes to us. Soon, your body and walking motion will feel weird when you don't have a ball at your feet.

Sometimes, it isn't even just a soccer ball. If you are walking down the street in a city, kick that bottle that you see lying on the ground. Better yet, challenge yourself and try to kick it into the garbage can. Make a game of it. Kick anything in sight (within reason, of course). Soccer players should be happy when something is at their feet. Juggle your rolled up socks. Kick around a tennis ball. The world is your soccer field and anything you can kick is your match ball.

Story: When I was in middle school, I was addicted to soccer. I ate, slept, and breathed the sport. So much so, that I would literally go to sleep with a ball at my feet. I would tuck in my sheets and roll a soccer ball down to my feet where I would keep it close to me. My body adapted, and soon I was so uncomfortable without a ball at my feet that I needed to take one everywhere I went. It became an extension of my body. That is the type of attitude that players need to have. Treat the soccer ball like an extension of yourself, and express how you feel with it. Let your feet do the writing in your book of life. And let the soccer ball be your pen.

9. Watch soccer as a student.

Of course, you can't constantly be on the soccer field working your butt off. There will be times when you are at home, relaxing on the couch. But those moments don't need to consist of wasted time. Remember, you can always be improving yourself. When you find yourself too tired to play, go into student mode. Soccer may not be a subject at your school, but it can be a subject in your life. Study the game. Create homework for yourself. Test yourself. Watch a game as a critic, and judge every move the players make. Making these types of observations while watching a game will make you more aware of your movements in a game. You will become more aware of situations that you are placed in because you have witnessed other players in the same scenarios.

Soccer isn't just a game, it is also a learning process. You can't just expect to become the best without studying. Soccer consists of patterns, moves, and strategies. The best players also make the best coaches, because they know the game inside and out. Knowledgeable players are easier to coach, and coachable players are highly sought after.

Story: When I was in elementary school, my dad bought me a movie called "2000 goals." It consisted of hours and hours just of players scoring goals in the English Premier League. I would watch it every single day. I literally memorized these players' moves and studied their finishes. Then, I would go outside and try to emulate every goal in the movie. I think I was such a prolific goal scorer because I saw all of these goals being scored, so I knew how to put the ball away in every scenario. I studied these goals so much that scoring became second nature to me.

10. Respect authority.

Every single coach you come across in your lifetime will be worth listening to. I guarantee it. Everyone has their own insight and their own strategies. Putting together the best advice you receive from every coach will give you a philosophy on the game that is worth writing a book about. Even if a coach is hard to understand, or even hard to like, respect him or her, and listen to every single word that comes out of his or her mouth. This is the best way to learn, and the best way to reach the next level.

Never clash heads with a coach. It will end up hurting you the most. Understand the fact that your coach is a coach for a reason, and you are a player for a reason. Do your job on the field, and the coach will do their job off of it. Other coaches and scouts take note of how respectful you are to authority, whether it's coaches or referees. People don't want to sign someone who complains and disregards everything a coach or ref says. It is also true that respect is earned. When you respect coaches, they will respect you back.

Story: I was always a player that listened to every word my coach said. Even off the field, at team dinners, I would channel in to his conversations and try and pick some advice out of what he said. I admired all of my coaches and I felt like I was always getting the best advice from them. It was like that until I got to college and I immediately clashed heads with my first head coach. He was always angry and I started to dislike him. Looking back, I think this period was when I improved the least, and I think it was because I didn't respect the coach. This was a college-level coach. So maybe if I had respected him, I would have gained a lot of knowledge. I learned that no matter how mean or tough a coach is, respect him, and listen to what he has to offer. You will learn, and you will grow.

11. Be loud!

Coaches love leaders. And leaders aren't afraid to be loud, assertive, and extroverted. Be loud off the field, and be loud on the field. Let your presence be felt no matter where you are. Lead with authority, and be heard. Coaches and teams all need leadership, and so that is a huge trait they look for in players. Look for every opportunity to direct your team and lead them in the right direction. Act like a symphony conductor. But instead of waving around your baton, use your voice to lead your team to success.

Also, always be sure that the content of what you are saying is reasonable and respectful. Being loud can also get you in trouble if you don't do it in the right way. Be loud, but also be positive. Being loud will make it easier for you to have impacts on your teammates and the game. Impactful players are usually the best of players. Your voice should be gone after every match, from motivating, screaming, and yelling. Make the opposing team know that you are there to support your teammates to the point of being annoying.

Story: When I was around the age of 10, we often played a team from a nearby city. They had a player who would never shut up on the field. He would just yell and yell and most of the time I had no idea what he was yelling. But I knew one thing: he was a leader. He wasn't the best of players, but he knew how to influence others, and coaches loved that. He ended up getting recruited to play division-1 college soccer. To be honest, I think it was just because he was a loud presence on the field. Be loud. It will get you noticed.

12. Eliminate unnecessary distractions.

Distractions come in all forms: video games, friends, food, or lost matches. It is crucial to figure out at an early age what is good for you and what is bad for you. Find out what is making you better, and what is holding you back from improvement. Imagine all of those distractions as actual weights that you are carrying around. Once you slowly start to eliminate all of those weights, it will be easier for you to progress and succeed. Not every distraction is unnecessary, but most of them are negative.

Distractions can also come from within one's mind. Distractions can be thoughts or feelings that are getting in the way of your success. You need to squish those thoughts and replace them with prosperous ones. Eliminating things from your life can be difficult, and it will suck at times, but you need to do it if you truly want to reach your dreams.

Story: I used to love Netflix. I could sit on Netflix all day and just browse through the films to see where I would indulge myself next. I quickly found out that time on Netflix was wasted time. If I didn't get rid of that distraction, I would soon be overweight, removed from soccer, and caught up in some sitcom that was completely irrelevant to me. I quickly eliminated that distraction and moved on with my life.

13. Be confident.

I can't express enough how key confidence is for being a professional athlete. Confidence is stepping up to the penalty spot in the 90th minute with the game on the line. Confidence is telling your coach your opinions that will better your chances of winning. Confidence is looking the journalist in the eyes and telling him that your team is going to win. Not everyone carries this trait, but everyone can gain it. Confidence is hard to attain, but you need to train your mind to believe in yourself.

However, confidence isn't just a thought, it is a train of thoughts. Confidence means constantly knowing that you will push through every task and that nothing can stop you. You will never become a professional soccer player if you don't carry confidence with you everywhere you go. Tell yourself that you will make it happen and you will be right. I have never met a pro soccer player who wasn't confident. You need to engrave it into your genes. You are amazing, and you can achieve all things.

Story: I wasn't confident in my childhood. But I trained myself to be confident. I would wake up every morning telling myself that I would be successful and I would be the best soccer player in the world. It may have never happened, but I had confidence that I could reach the top. No matter what anyone said to me, I believed I would be successful at everything I did. I was taught that the more confidence I have, the harder it will be for an opposing player to get in my head and knock me down. Have confidence in yourself, or else nobody will.

14. Be mentally strong.

Being mentally strong and being confident are not the same. Being confident means you think no one can touch you. Being mentally strong means you won't let anyone touch you. You have to be mentally strong because you will take a beat down day in and day out, and you have to be prepared to deal with a lot of disrespect and hatred. Mentally strong players are the ones that get taken down in the box 5 times in a game without a single penalty call, and still manage to keep their head on straight and fight for a goal in the dying seconds. Mentally strong players can face the toughest team in the league, and still convince their teammates that they can win the game.

Being mentally strong shouldn't just be a trait on the field, but also in life. How much of a beating can you take, and still push forward with your head held high? I dare you to put yourself in a position that makes you fight. Mentally strong people don't even flinch when put in a scenario that brings them discomfort. Mental strength will propel you to where you want to be, even more so than physical strength.

Story: Growing up, I was weak mentally. I took beat down after beat down from teachers, opposing players, bullies, and everyone that wanted to hold me back from my dreams. I built strength over time. Sometimes, the strongest people mentally are the ones who went through hell and managed to come out on top. I didn't let anyone hold me back, and I kept my eyes on the prize. Now, I love when a person talks down to me, or when something bad is written about me. It runs through my mind as "if you only knew how wrong you are" and I simply laugh. I've heard it all before; so don't let people faze you. Actually, it can be your best motivation.

15. Be physically strong.

Although mental strength is more important than physical strength, don't let yourself turn soft. As the levels of soccer get higher, so does the physicality of the leagues. Never let yourself fall behind. Hit the gym at least three times a week, working on every single muscle and slowly building yourself up to a player that every opponent fears. Make it a goal to be the player that the opposing team looks at before the game and thinks, "Crap, this is going to be a long game." Be the player that is impossible to push off the ball. Be the player that makes your teammates glad you are on their team and not the other.

Treat your workouts like you treat a game. Take them very seriously and always put all of your effort forward. It wouldn't hurt to ask your coach or a personal trainer for a program that you can follow. There are also programs on the Internet that are used by professional soccer players around the world. Being physically strong is proven to build self-confidence as well, and that doesn't hurt either. But no matter what, don't be a weak link on the team. Always look to increase weight and increase reps in your workout routine.

Story: When I was in college, my coach found out that I was going to the gym outside of his practice. I got called into his office and they said that if I didn't stop working out so much, they weren't going to let me play. He felt insulted because he felt that his training program wasn't enough for me. I apologized, and promised him I would take it easy. However, I just started going to the gym late at night when I knew no one would catch me.

16. Listen to music.

This advice may be a little weird to you. You may be thinking, "What does this have to do with soccer?" I promise you though, connect yourself with music. Everyone needs to shut the world out every once in a while. Whether it is to pump you up before a long game, or to calm you down after a tough loss, find music and create playlists for every mood. Music is a positive way to connect to your emotions. It speaks to you when you don't want to speak to anyone else. It is known as the athlete's therapist. No one will judge you for the music you listen to because nobody has to know.

Soccer is filled with long bus rides and long days of anxiety and nerves. Sometimes, it is best to just put on some headphones and imagine yourself scoring ten goals and winning the game without a problem. Music is also known to push soccer players to improve stamina. Go for a run without music and then go for a run listening to your favorite jams. I guarantee you'll go longer and feel better when listening to that music. Then, since you can't listen to music on the field, listen to those same songs before a game and get them stuck in your head. You will run a lot longer than you would in silence. Music helps you reach your inner peace in your hard times, and your soccer stardom in your game times.

Story: In high school, I did not like sitting in silence. Feeling the nerves run through my body before a big game and have nothing to clear my mind was a struggle that I needed to get rid of. Then, my good ol' friend Eminem came along and all of a sudden I found myself scoring goals left and right. I blasted music before games so that when I got onto the field, it was all I could hear. I slowly built my fitness up and wasn't tired towards the end of games anymore. Having that little bit of motivation singing in the back of your mind will help you more than you think.

17. Stay busy.

Between soccer and school, there are still going to be times when you just sit around, praying time would speed up and you would be back on the soccer field playing under the lights. My advice: don't. Don't ever wish to speed time up. But rather, take advantage of your time and stay busy. Stay busy improving yourself. Time is supposed to be spent wisely. And you will drive yourself crazy if you have all this free time and you just waste it hoping that one day you will be playing in the English Premier League. The busier you are, the more you will improve.

If you have some free time, turn on some soccer, go outside and kick a soccer ball, go for a run. Fill your schedule and don't let a second go to waste. Only boring people get bored. Don't be boring. Be a dream chaser and stay busy. Successful people wake up early because this allows their days to be longer. Successful people stay busy because they are always looking to achieve new goals. The busier you are, the less distractions you will face. However, don't confuse movement with progress. Just because you are doing something doesn't mean you are getting closer to the end goal. Stay busy, but also stay smart with your time.

Story: In college, my teammates were always asking me to go out to parties or go drinking with them. My "stay busy" strategy allowed me to stay focused on my end goal of becoming a pro. I made sure I was always busy, but I also made it clear to them by putting together a schedule that I put on my dorm room door. I had a list of everything I had to do, whether it was the gym, homework, studying, or watching film. They started asking me less and less, and I was able to avoid going out with them altogether. Staying busy is positive for multiple reasons. Staying busy has kept me away from many distractions through out my career.

18. Reach out to potential connections.

Soccer is a lot like the real world when your career is starting out. It is not about what you know. It is about who you know. Politics are a big part of the soccer world. And although you may not like it, you need to embrace it and start networking and connecting. Create a dedicated email and use it to reach out to coaches or professional players for advice. Also, start to add more people on Facebook, Instagram, or any other social networking platforms. Getting yourself known is sometimes just as important as getting to know others. Build your address book and stay connected with people who will one day be able to connect you to your dream job.

Treat every relationship like a stepping-stone. The more people you know, the more opportunities you are subconsciously creating for yourself. Respect everyone, as you never know who may just be that key to opening the next door for you. Always be on the lookout for people who are interested in chasing the same dreams as you. Key connections aren't always coaches or scouts. Sometimes, other players are the ones that can hook you up with a tryout or an opportunity that you never would have gotten on your own. And when this happens, be thankful and stay connected. Never burn bridges. Make yourself accessible and people will come to you.

Story: I, like many other people, receive a lot of weird Facebook friend requests. But I never judge people, so I usually end up adding them anyways. Believe it or not, while I was training in Europe fighting for my first professional contract, I accepted one of those random friend requests. That person ended up being a general manager for a team in Sweden and had heard about me. He referred me to a friend of his, who gave me a tryout with his team. That led to my first-ever professional contract. My dreams came true thanks to connections. Get connected!

19. Record yourself playing.

You are not always in the same place as the team you want to play for. How do you think that team is going to know how good you are when you are halfway across the country, or even across the world? This is when modern-day technology is a lifesaver. Record yourself playing any way possible, even if it is on your grandfather's flip phone. You can be the best player in the world, but if no one has seen you play, then you are screwed. People need to know how good you are. Video footage will help propel your career into the right direction. Also, don't just record the good stuff. Make sure you have full-game footage. Coaches want to see your 90-minute effort, not just your easy finishes and goal celebrations against the worst team in the league.

When you do get the necessary footage, send it to everyone. Send it to every college coach that you know. Send it to professional teams across the world. Send it to soccer agencies. You should even put it on YouTube and email the URL to people. Have some confidence and take some chances. You will never know what opportunities or responses you may receive. Let the world know how good you are.

Story: In my junior and senior years of high school, I had footage of all of my goals and assists. I put them together into a highlight film and sent them to my top 30 college choices. I got responses from Notre Dame, Duke, Indiana, and many other top soccer universities. I was from a small town in Wisconsin, but my highlight video opened my capabilities up to the best universities in the country. I strongly encourage you to film your games. Knowing you are being filmed will also motivate you to push for perfection. But don't worry if you trip over the ball, you can always edit that part out.

20. Follow a strict diet plan.

Even though you are still young and feel like you can eat whatever you want, be careful with what you put into your body. Try and stay away from fast food restaurants and anything else that is high in fats or sugars. Although they may seem like they aren't slowing you down now, they will hurt you in the future. Getting into a routine of eating unhealthy foods will create a hard habit to break. I have seen too many players come back from the off-season 15-20 pounds overweight, because they didn't have the self-control to stay away from candies and hamburgers.

Dieting can be the hardest part of a successful career and a healthy body. But if you really want to become a professional soccer player, you need to take it seriously. Your diet should be a high protein plan. Take away potato chips and Oreos and replace them with meats, fruits, vegetables, or nuts. Treat your body like a temple. After all, your body may be what makes you a lot of money in the future, so treat it right. You don't fill a racecar with soda. You fill it with what it needs to drive quickly. What are you going to choose for your fuel?

Story: When I got to high school, I knew I had to take my diet seriously. However, I didn't have much education, aside from knowing that I had to eat a lot of protein. I only looked at protein contents on the packaging of foods and drinks. I would drink a gallon of chocolate milk a day, and I would eat peanut butter by the spoonful. Little did I know, this wasn't the greatest option for my health. After gaining some weight, I decided to do some hardcore research, and soon noticed that I had to look at content other than just protein. That was unfortunate because I was really starting to enjoy all that chocolate milk.

21. Build your social media presence.

With how far social media has come nowadays, building your presence is a must. Get as many Twitter followers, Facebook friends, and Instagram followers as possible, and make yourself well-known. This may not seem like it is doing you any good, but down the road it will definitely come in handy. Make sure you only post positive things about yourself and your career. People will start to pay attention and your name may start to get thrown around in conversations. Many opportunities can come from having a big social media presence. Believe it or not, some coaches and agents will have more interest in you if they see you are able to attract people to games and sell tickets. They often check the social media profiles of potential players.

With that being said, stay away from posting statuses in the moment! Too many times has a player posted something negative or controversial and ended up losing the interest of teams or even getting fined. Always double check your posts before you press "enter." Refrain from swearing, accusing, or offensive slurs that you wouldn't want your own mother to read. Instead, post your gratitude. Post pictures of you after a big win. Show the world that you are a great person who will continue to do great things.

Story: In college, I had consistently posted about how dissatisfied I was with my coach and my lack of playing time. I tweeted about how badly I wanted to transfer and get off campus as soon as I could. Well, my coach had full access to all of my social media accounts, and I had no idea. In my end-of-season meeting with the coach, he had printouts of all of these posts and displayed them on his desk. I immediately knew I was in trouble. You could say I was a little embarrassed.

22. Ask questions.

It never hurts to be curious. No matter how stupid you may feel, you will always feel better after you find out the answer to a question of yours, so ask it. The only stupid question is the one that you are too scared to ask. You can never have too much knowledge when it comes to soccer, so squeeze every last bit of it out of everyone that you know within the sport. You will never be the smartest soccer expert, and so that is why you should always be asking questions. Figure out why your coach wants you to make a certain run. Ask why your goalkeeper prefers to dive to his left instead of his right. Ask why your coach thinks your team plays better with a 4-4-2 formation instead of a 4-3-3. The more knowledge you build, the better soccer player you will become.

Don't just ask questions of others. Start to ask questions to yourself. Ask yourself why you run a certain way or why you decided your pass was the best decision. Start to analyze the way you play and you will start to notice errors that you are now conscious enough to fix. When you start to get to the higher levels of soccer, in college and the pros, set up meetings with your coaches and teammates. Be on a constant search for knowledge. Start to create your own soccer philosophy and soon people will be asking you questions for your opinions. Build your brain.

Story: I was always the quiet player on the team in elementary school. I just played soccer and didn't think much of it. Then, one day, I noticed one of my teammates having an intellectual conversation with our coach about soccer. They were talking about wall passes and overlaps and I had no idea what was going on. From that day on, I started Googling soccer terminology and asking more questions at practice. I was determined to become a soccer guru. I still Google terms and bombard my coaches with curiosities to this day.

23. Build friendships with teammates.

It is rare that you will like every single teammate in your life. But there are many positives to forming close friendships. Coaches and scouts can tell when certain players aren't likable simply by watching how they are around their teammates. If you are always bickering or arguing with teammates, coaches will immediately lose interest. Building a bond with your teammates will also make you more comfortable on the field. It will make games and practices more enjoyable because you aren't just playing with your teammates. You are also playing with your friends.

On top of the comfort and enjoyment, having trust within a team always adds to the success. Having teammates that trust you and are constantly making an effort to get you the ball will make you look more attractive to scouts. Being friends with your teammates also allows you to hang out with them off the field and stay out of trouble. You can go outside and practice together while also having a good time just hanging out and talking. Become friends with your teammates because your teammates understand you and can relate to you on so many levels.

Story: I think I improved more in high school than I did in college because of who I was friends with. In high school, I was friends with all of my soccer teammates and so we would all hang out and kick the ball around. At the time I was just having fun, but I was subconsciously improving my skills by getting so many touches on the ball with them. Then, I got to college and had no friends at all. I wasn't able to call anybody to go to the park and kick the ball around. When I was a friend of my teammates, they tried to get me the ball every time it was at their feet and I would reciprocate as well. There is a huge difference between being friends and being teammates.

24. Believe in yourself.

Having confidence in yourself is a daily thing. However, believing in yourself is taking a look at the big picture and knowing you are going to become a professional soccer player. Put aside all of the daily routines and goals. Believe that you are doing everything you are doing for a purpose. Believe in that purpose. You were put on this earth to play professional soccer and you are going to do just that. Be confident that you can win your next game, but also believe that you are going to one-day change the world. Believe that you are going to one-day play in front of 50,000 fans in a sold-out stadium. Don't ever let that belief fade.

Your belief should be contagious. You should never be alone when it comes to believing that you are going to make it as a pro. If you truly believe in yourself, then others will believe in you too. Make everyone in your life aware that you are going to one day become a professional soccer player. Walk around with your chest out and never hesitate when someone asks you what your future holds. Have the ability to look people in the eyes and say, "I am going to be a professional soccer player."

Story: I have had the same answer since I was 8-years-old to the question, "What do you want to be when you grow up?' I have always believed in myself because I knew I deserved it. I knew that if I put in the work and kept my eyes on the prize, I could become a professional soccer player. One of the best feelings I have is knowing that I was able to prove my 8-year-old self right. When your belief is strong enough, no one can touch or sway it. Just believe.

25. Accept failures.

Nothing comes easy in the journey to becoming a professional soccer player. There will be plenty of victories, but the failures that you face are what will be important. Success in the soccer world is achieved by how you act. But that success is sustained by how you react. Learn to accept failures and use them as motivation. Hold onto poor evaluations from coaches at soccer camps. Keep videos of games that you lost 3-0. Keep those memories in the back of your head and think to yourself, "Never again."

You will try and there will be times that you fail. Even Lionel Messi and Cristiano Ronaldo get shut down sometimes. The best soccer players are the ones that can bounce back after a defeat and work that much harder. If you never lose, then you never learn. Accept failures and analyze them. Think about what you did wrong and how you can improve. On and off the soccer field, you are guaranteed failure through out life. So don't be surprised when it happens. Prepare yourself for victory, but learn to be okay with failure. With that being said, avoid failure at all costs. It sucks.

Story: I have hundreds of newspaper articles saved from my high school, college, and professional career. Almost all of them have my name in the headline and have come after a victory. I love looking through them and remembering how fun it was to score all those goals. But I think the most important article I kept was of a game we lost 1-0, which is a huge embarrassment for any striker. Losing 1-0 is a slap to the face, because if I had scored just one goal, then the result would have been different. But I've learned to accept my failures and learn from them. That failure made me promise to myself to never lose a game 1-0 again. To this day, I have kept that promise. Avoid failing, but learn to accept the inevitable.

26. Wake up early.

Time and time again you will hear successful people say in interviews that one of their biggest keys to success is waking up early and attacking the day. I have noticed that this is exactly the case as well when you talk with successful soccer players. Sleep is very important for your health, but too much sleep is a waste of time. Go to bed at a reasonable time, and wake up when the sun rises. Take full advantage of the light. Don't be one of those teenagers who sleeps until noon and doesn't get going until half the day is already over. Sleeping in is easy. Sleeping in is for the lazy. Don't be lazy.

If you are having difficulty waking up early, set an alarm for an early-morning workout session. Don't come up with excuses. "I don't feel good. I'll do it tomorrow." I have heard that way too many times. Your chances of becoming a professional soccer player can be improved by finding time to train outside of normal team practices and this is a key way to find that personal training time. Don't sleep in and miss out on your opportunity. Jump out of bed excited to attack the day. Make yourself a nice hardy breakfast and go improve yourself.

Story: I was stuck in a routine my freshman year of high school of sleeping in until noon on the weekends. Getting too much sleep made me even more tired and I ended up usually wasting the rest of my days just lying around. I woke up early one Saturday because I heard a door shut downstairs. I looked out my window to see my mom and dad going for a walk together as the sun wasn't even up yet. How dare my parents have more motivation than me! They were like a hundred years old and I was just a teenager. I quickly got dressed and ran after them. I made it a point every morning on the weekends to get up early and go for a walk with them. That little bit of motivation extended my days by 4 or more hours and I felt more alive than ever. Do yourself a favor and get your butt out of bed.

27. Lose excuse habits.

Do you want to know what coaches hate more than losing? Excuses. Even as a player, I strongly dislike listening to my teammates after a game whine about the refs not making a call or a teammate not making a pass. It is brutally annoying. Don't be that guy. The world is the way it is and sometimes you just have to focus on what you can change. There is no point in coming up with excuses for things that are out of your control. As for things that are in your control, just apologize and move on. It is tiring to constantly be thinking of an excuse as to why something didn't go your way. Look forward and just make it go your way next time.

From this moment on, I challenge you to never come up with another excuse for as long as you live. If you are late to practice, apologize and promise that it won't happen again. If you miss a shot, don't tell your coach that the ball took a weird bounce. Sometimes, you don't even need to explain yourself, so an excuse isn't worth it. Just understand that you messed up and move on. The people that spend time thinking of excuses are the ones who miss out on time for preparation. Let the past be the past and prepare for the future.

Story: I had a really hard-nosed coach when I was towards the end of my teenage years. He told it how it was and never hesitated to speak his mind. I remember him cutting one of our best players from the team right after tryouts. I was standing right next to him when the conversation happened. The coach looked the player dead in the eyes after being questioned why the player got cut and replied, "I just got sick and tired of hearing all your bull shit excuses." My jaw dropped and I quickly turned away to avoid any awkwardness. Hearing that come from a coach has made me scared to even think about coming up with excuses. Lesson learned.

28. Brand yourself.

Who are you? Better yet, what do represent? It is your time to start acting like a marketing expert. What is your style of play? What are your strengths? What type of hairstyle are you known for? What number do you wear on the soccer field? What type or color of shoes do you wear? What is your swag? Grab a pen and paper and start writing down the answers to all of these questions. Write down what you want people to see when they look at you.

Once you have done this, stick to that persona for the rest of your life. You want people to see your jersey number in public and think of you. You want people to see someone else with your hairstyle and think of you. Create your brand and run with it. Market yourself on social media and in public and make your brand known. Coaches want players who can bring in attendance and gain fans. Are you exciting enough to sell tickets? Is your brand unique enough to stand out in public? Create your own uniqueness and stand out from the rest. Don't settle for fitting in with the rest of the crowd. Be the player that stands out on a soccer field. Be weird. Be exciting. Be worth buying a season ticket for.

Story: I played professional indoor soccer for a couple years as a hobby to stay busy during my winters in America. My coach approached me and told me that I needed to stand out more. I was unsure what he meant by this, so I interpreted it the best I could. I dyed my hair bleach blonde and bought myself bright pink indoor game boots. From that day on, I had no trouble sticking out and the fans loved it. I created my brand and from that day forward I had crazy hair and bright shoes. I topped it off as a speedy player with fancy footwork and I sold plenty of tickets. People wanted to see my unique brand. Creating myself helped boost my career and increase my contract worth.

29. Smile!

Positivity draws positivity. You probably think smiling isn't going to help you become a professional soccer player. In that case, we can agree to disagree. Being noticeably happy draws people to you and it draws attraction. It is the same way with people of the opposite gender. If you smile more, people will find you more attractive and it'll be easier to find a boyfriend or girlfriend. It works the same way with coaches in soccer. Coaches don't want negative grumpy players to play for them. They want people who can spread joy through out the team, even in the hard times. Coaches are drawn to players who are always smiling. For example, you can't hate Ronaldinho. He was always the happiest player on the field and fans loved that about him.

A smile a day brings the scouts your way. Maybe not exactly, but being open and happy towards scouts or coaches will make them feel more comfortable to be around you. It is easy to associate yourself with someone who is always smiling. People enjoy that type of positivity in their life. Being happy is contagious. A happier you will lead to happier teammates, happier coaches, and a happier team. Happiness brings positive thoughts and positive thoughts lead to a winning attitude.

Story: I have always had fun playing soccer. No matter how serious or intense the game was, I was having a good time. I'm always smiling and laughing on the field. When I was in high school, a college coach approached me and gave me his business card. He said, "We could use more players who enjoy the game as much as you do." Then he walked away. He didn't compliment my goal-scoring ability. He didn't compliment my speed. The main thing he noticed was that I was happy, smiling, and enjoying the beautiful game. That moment really stuck with me.

30. Never fade from a tackle.

Fear is a dangerous thing on the soccer field. I absolutely hate it when a player goes into a tackle without full effort. How could you not want the ball? Why would you not put everything you have into winning the ball? Possessing the ball is how you win soccer games. You can't score if you don't have the ball. Look at every tackle as a goal-scoring opportunity. If you win the ball for your team, then your team now has the chance to put the ball in the back of the net. Always fight for the ball.

Coaches tend to stay away from shy or weak players. They don't want players who aren't going to put their bodies on the line. Scouts notice every move you make. They will know when you don't go 100% into a tackle. You are practically giving the ball to the other team. Winning a hard tackle will definitely grab a scout's attention. Treat every tackle as a make-or-break situation for your career. Either you lose it and your strength is questioned, or you win it and people want you on their team.

Story: I was on a trial with a Swedish team and was working as hard as I could to score goals. I threw my body at every cross and I shot from every angle. I was scoring goal after goal in one of our scrimmages. I thought I was doing so well and my confidence was growing. Then, one of my teammates lost the ball and I tried to get the ball back but I shied away from the hard challenge. I thought I had to put all my effort into scoring goals, not winning tackles. I was a striker. Then, the coach called me over right away and asked, "What was that?" I responded, "What was what?" He told me that weak challenges aren't accepted on his team. Being a forward, I had never considered adding "strong tackler" to my strengths and abilities. I ended up not getting offered a contract. Never again will I shy away from a tackle.

31. Build relationships with coaches.

Building friendships with teammates is important, but building relationships with your coaches is beyond crucial. Every coach you have will be a reference for the rest of your life. Don't be surprised when a college coach calls your high school coach and asks how you are as a player and as a student. Also don't be surprised when your high school coach tells the truth. The relationships you form with your coaches will help you and your career grow. Coaches who like you will make sure they teach you and expand your game. Coaches who don't like you will make sure you help their team win and that's it. Treat every coach as a mentor that you respect.

If you disagree with your coach, don't ever argue. The best way to handle disagreements is by asking him or her why they think that way and look at the situation from their point-of-view. You should view your coaches as critical parts of your personal success. Don't betray them. Don't lie to them. Don't disrespect them. Give them your full attention and learn from them. Make them enjoy having you as a player. The best type of player is a coachable player. Get close with your coaches and your career will prosper.

Story: I was spoiled as a very young child because my youth soccer coach was my father until I was 12-years-old. Not only did this help me learn the game, but this also taught me to respect my coaches. I would never mistreat my own dad, even if I disagreed with his coaching technique. I carried that attitude with me through out my whole career. I have respected every coach of mine like a father. I have gotten very close with most of my coaches because I know that I can learn so much from each and every one of them. These coach-player relationships will be some of the best relationships through out your life.

32. Win more, but lose better.

Nobody likes a sore loser. Some soccer players have the attitude that winning is everything. I don't necessarily disagree with them. Unfortunately, those people who accept nothing but winning are the ones who are whining and pouting after a loss. You can't go undefeated every season. You can't win every single game for the rest of your life. Learn to walk off the field after a loss and be proud because you gave everything you could towards trying to win the game. Congratulate the other team. Thank the referees for their time. Then walk into the locker room and encourage your team to keep on fighting. Learn that there is always a new day.

As a teenager, it can be expected that your emotions are flying high and times are frustrating. However, I can guarantee that when a scout is at your game, they don't stop watching once the final whistle blows. They keep their eyes on you until the very last second that you are in their sight. Never let your emotions get the best of you. Approach every game to win, but approach every loss to learn. Be a positive loser. The losses will come and go but the lessons you learn from those losses will stick with you forever. So don't be frustrated that you lost, be grateful that you improved.

Story: I hated losing. I hated losing more than I loved winning. I would cry after losses and refuse to shake the opposing team's hands. But I learned at an early age that I looked pathetic, thanks to my dad recording even after the final whistle. I saw myself on camera being a sore loser and I thought I was ugly, spoiled, and annoying. My dad taught me that losses aren't the end of the world. I will wake up the next day with a new opportunity to chase victory. So now, when I lose, I thank the referees and I congratulate the other team. Then I wait until I'm in private to yell at the top of my lungs. But then I move on.

33. Never skip leg day.

There are so many players that have these huge biceps and broad shoulders, and they think that is enough to be strong on the soccer field. News flash - those bench presses are not going to win championships. You may look tough, but a player with a strong lower body always beats a player with a strong upper body in a tackle. Lower your center of gravity and you will be quicker and stronger. Squats are a soccer player's savior. Building your leg muscles prevents injuries in your knees, ankles, and hips.

Always spend at least a couple days a week busting your butt at the gym, literally. Squats, leg presses, calf raises, leg extensions, and any other exercises that build lower body strength, do them. Work with resistance training by using stretchy bands to enhance your quickness and speed. Most injuries in soccer occur from lack of muscle strength and tendons or ligaments giving out. It is hard to improve your game when you are injured and spending your time on the sidelines. Avoid this time off by putting time in. Your gym is your friend. Again, Google lower body routines or hire a personal trainer. Your legs are your career.

Story: I skipped one too many leg days and that is why I have torn my ACL twice. My doctor told me that my quadriceps weren't strong enough to keep up with the amount of stress I was putting on them. Therefore, when my quad muscles were too weak, my knee gave out and I tore some ligaments. Ever since those injuries, I have made sure that I never skip a leg day at the gym. I can't stress enough how important it is to invest time to building your lower body muscle mass. Always choose lower body over upper body. Don't become top heavy. You will tip over, along with your career.

34. Run your butt off.

Don't just spend time lifting weights at the gym. Hit the treadmill or go for a run. Fitness is every soccer player's worst nightmare, but it is a necessity for a successful career. I don't care if you're a defender, midfielder, forward, or even a goalkeeper. Build your fitness and become a box-to-box player. Box-to-box players are so well paid and such a necessity because there are so few of them. Set challenges and goals consistently to push your stamina to new limits. Try and run everyday. Using goals will make it more interesting, and don't forget to listen to music!

Most of the best moments in soccer history have occurred in the final 10 minutes of a soccer match. The players that are still able to run the full length of the field and bust their butts to win a ball in the 90th minute are the players that coaches want on their team. Don't be a player that huffs and puffs after a 10-yard sprint in the final minutes of the game. If you want to make yourself desirable, build your fitness. Even if you aren't technically talented, being fit will make you an attraction to lots of coaches.

Story: No soccer player hates fitness more than I do. I strongly believe that. And it wasn't until I got to college that I realized how important it really was. I never ran much in high school, but college quickly changed that. The first day of practice in college was the Cooper test, where we were forced to run 2 miles in 12 minutes. I never had a chance. Since I didn't complete the test, I was forced to sit out the first match. And I absolutely hated sitting on the bench. I knew that things had to change, so I made a goal to run 4 miles in 24 minutes. Not only did my fitness improve, but I also started to score more goals towards the end of matches. Push yourself when it comes to fitness. You can never have too much.

35. Hydrate.

Most teenagers don't take hydration seriously because it is just something your middle school health teacher tells you to maintain. Well actually, your middle school health teacher may have given you some excellent advice. If you really want to play professional soccer one day, you must train frequently. In order to train frequently, you need to keep your body well maintained. The best way to keep your body healthy is to drink as much water as possible. Doctors will tell the average person to drink at least 8 glasses a day. But remember, you are far from average. Try doubling that. If you really push yourself, you will be sweating buckets each and every day.

Always keep a water bottle on you. Never put yourself in a scenario where water isn't easily accessible. It should be forbidden for a player to suffer a cramp, because a cramp is your body screaming for hydration. Treat your body with the respect it deserves. Your body is going to make you a lot of money one day, but only if you keep it hydrated. Also, stay away from sodas, sugar-filled juices, and of course alcohols. Instead, try to make your own smoothies with natural fruits.

Story: I have suffered one cramp in my life. I had the ball in the box and was about to fire a shot on goal. Right when I planted my foot, my calf locked up completely and I fell to the ground. That cramp really hurt. It left me on the ground for at least a minute. And worst of all, it took away a goal scoring opportunity. After that, I focused on hydration to assure that this would not happen again. I don't understand how anyone would let his or her body get to that point. Do yourself a favor and keep your body hydrated. Cramps stop goal scoring. Down with cramps!

36. Just say, "No."

It is sad that I need to add this to the guide, but I have seen drugs end way too many soccer careers. Being the soccer star of your school, people are going to want to be with you and influence you. Don't ever think any kind of drug is okay. Drugs will ruin your brain, ruin your career, and ruin you. Get into the habit of just saying, "No." You don't need any excuses. You don't need to come up with any specific reasons. Just say, "No," and avoid it at all costs. Temptation and peer pressure are very common, especially in high school.

Keeping yourself on the right path should always be your motivation for staying away from drugs. One bad decision and your whole life can change for the worse. Put yourself in the right crowd, and stay clean. Friends that offer you drugs are not true friends. It's either professional soccer or drugs, and I'm sure you will make the right decision.

Story: One of my close friends used to be the best-behaved and most innocent kids I had ever known. He had an early curfew and never put himself in harm's way. That was until high school. He was one of the best players on varsity as a freshman, and got into the wrong crowd. His first time trying marijuana was with a couple of his teammates in a car. Sure enough, a couple of cops pulled them over and busted all of them. Even though it was his first offense, his reputation was stained. His chances of playing in college were ruined just because he made one stupid choice. He could have just said, "No." His career would probably still be prosperous and he would be happy. But that is proof that one bad choice can ruin everything. Be safe and be smart.

37. Be selfish.

Now don't take this the wrong way, but selfishness will get you to where you want to be. I do not mean selfishness by hogging the ball and shooting every time you touch it. I mean selfishness when it comes to your well-being and your career. Be selfish and put your happiness before everything else. Do what makes you happy and what is going to get you to your dreams. Don't ever let someone get in the way of your life. Live your life for YOU! Chase your dreams for YOU. Put yourself first and do whatever it takes to get to your final destination.

When it comes to being on the soccer field, selfishness within reason is always a bonus for a soccer player. Be selfish and take the penalty kick. Be selfish and demand the ball to win the game in the final minutes. Be selfish and know that you are the guy or girl that the team is looking at to win the game. Selfishness is only handy with confidence. When you are selfish, you better back it up. When you have the ball and a 2-on-1 breakaway, shoot. If you are confident, then be selfish. No one will be mad at you for scoring.

Story: When I finished my first year of college soccer, I wanted to go to Europe to try and get a professional contract. I started looking up plane tickets, and suddenly everyone and everything tried getting in my way. My teammates thought I wasn't ready. My family members thought it was a bad idea. Friends didn't want me to leave. But I knew this was a moment I needed to be selfish. I pushed everyone else's interests aside and did what was best for me, and my happiness. I went to Europe, and guess what. I earned that professional contract. Be selfish and go get what you have been focusing on and working for. You deserve it.

38. Stay after practice.

Dedication is easy to detect. Are you truly dedicated? The best way to judge dedication is to watch and see what they do when coach dismisses practice. Most players take off their cleats and shin guards and call it a day. Are you like most players? Don't be. Just because team practice is over doesn't mean your personal practice is over. Think of practice as a warm up for your own practice. Coaches can only push the team to the weakest link's breaking point. If you aren't the weakest link on your team, then stay after practice and push yourself to your limits. The best players are the last ones to leave.

Always go to practice prepared to stay afterwards. Bring some extra balls. Bring some cones. Ask any of your teammates if they want to stay later. You can even ask your coach if he or she wants to stay a little later and give you personal lessons. If you train the same amount as everyone else, you will stay at their level. Never settle for mediocrity. Get as far away from it as possible. Play until it gets dark out. And when it gets dark, use your car lights and keep playing.

Story: In high school, I was always the last player to leave the field. I bought myself 10 extra soccer balls and would bring them to every practice prepared to train on my own after practice. In pre-season, we had two-a-days every day. The first practice started at 9 AM and the second was at 3 PM. I would stay after the morning practice and train all the way until the second practice began. The coach was impressed with me because I was always so "early" to the second practice. Little did he know: I never went home.

39. Treat practices like championships.

Prepare for every practice like it is life or death. The best way to improve at training is to take it seriously. Before practice, eat a healthy meal and stay hydrated. Mentally prepare yourself to win every exercise. Push yourself to finish each technical exercise perfectly and minimize all mistakes. Have the attitude that you need to win every single challenge in practice, no matter the severity of it. Push yourself, and encourage your teammates. Lead by example and lead with positivity. Put your body on the line. Your teammates will think you are crazy, but they should also know that your effort is making them better as well.

If you are lazy at practice and don't take it seriously, then your body will make that adjustment and you won't be as prepared for games. Practice is meant for improvement and you can't improve if you aren't pushing your limits and expanding your boundaries. Don't leave the practice field with any effort left to give. Don't be one of those players that goes all-out in games, but barely puts in any effort at practice. Those players may be good at the moment, but they won't improve and become the best that they can be.

Story: I am way too competitive to take practice lightly. No matter the game or exercise, I would risk my life trying to win it. My teammates started to get angry with me because they thought they were going to get hurt. One practice, we had a youth coach from England come to our club and give a training session. As usual, I was the one kid that was sprinting the whole time, going in for every tackle. After the practice my coach told me that the English coach said I would be the only player that would make it playing in Europe. Ten years later that coach was right. And since my first training session, I realized why Europe is so far ahead of America in the soccer world. Every player treats every practice like a World Cup match.

40. Read coaching books.

You may plan on never coaching a day of soccer in your life. But coaching books aren't just for coaches. Coaches aren't the only students of the game. Players should study the game more so than coaches, because they are the ones executing moves on the field. Coaching books will teach you about strategies, philosophies, and advice necessary to be at the highest level in the world. Reading these books will give you knowledge that you won't get by just playing the game. You will gain a whole new dimension of understanding that you never even knew existed. You will begin to find yourself looking at games differently and reading the game from a different point-of-view.

Also, just because you are a player, doesn't mean you can't be a coach on the field. That is pretty much the job of a team captain: to lead the team where the coach cannot. A captain must understand coaching techniques, and be able to direct a team. The best players are able to read how a game is being played and adjust, not just themselves, but the whole team on the fly. Reading coaching books will bring out the true leader in you, because you will then be more knowledgeable and comfortable leading your team in games.

Story: As a player, I hated reading, but I loved leading. I had to make the sacrifice and dedicate myself to reading books about coaching and leadership. I set a goal of reading at least one book a month on the topic of coaching. At the time, I didn't want to be a coach in the future, but I wanted the knowledge that coaches had. I slowly started to see my thoughts change during games. Before, they were complete chaos. But then, they became more developed and detailed. I started understanding why certain things were happening. This allowed me to be one step ahead of every other player at all times.

41. Grade yourself.

Self-assessments are an ideal way to understand one's own improvements, strengths, and opportunities. Create a system for grading your own performance after every single practice and game. Create a spreadsheet listing categories such as finishing, passing, dribbling, defending, and leading. After every performance, grade yourself from 1-10. Then, next to every grade, leave some space for notes. Add any thoughts or opinions you have about your performance in that notes section. Keep track of every single report sheet you create. You need to go back through these reports at the end of every month and see if you are improving, or if you are heading in the wrong direction.

Don't be too harsh, but also don't go too easy on yourself. You must be giving your honest opinion. No one else has to see these reports. The notes section will also be beneficial when you go back and read through them. Understanding your own strengths and weaknesses makes it easier to improve your game overall. You can even write these assessments, and then go back and watch the film to see if you have missed anything. It is always good to get multiple views of how you play.

Story: I started creating self-assessments when I was in high school. I was forced to pay close attention to my abilities and I had never known how badly I needed to work on my defending. It wasn't until I made these assessments that I realized my defensive game was almost non-existent. I had a hard time grading myself, because I was never really put in a defensive position. I then made sure that I tracked back on defense a lot more and went in for more tackles, just so that I would have a defensive effort to grade. If I never had made these self-assessments, I probably still would have no defensive ability whatsoever.

42. Write your thoughts.

Along with the self-assessments, you should be writing down opinions and thoughts even relating to life off of the soccer field. You may find it handy to always have a pen and small notebook on you at all times when you think of a smart motivational speech for your team or maybe a new move you want to start practicing. The brain is a mystery and at times it can be brilliant. Always be prepared to write down thoughts that come to mind. Build a relationship with yourself and become aware of your own thought processes. Become your own psychologist. This way, you are always self-conscious and can adjust your mind to different scenarios.

Many people find writing down thoughts beneficial because it makes us always aware of what is going on around us. Awareness is a huge positive trait when it comes to soccer players. Writing down your thoughts turns you into an observer. Soccer players need to know what is going on around them at all times, because that is what a soccer game calls for. There is always action going on all around you, and you need to adjust to that action. Be aware of your own thoughts, and be aware of your surroundings. If you can boost your awareness, then you will own the soccer field.

Story: I always thought that journals and diaries were too girly for a man to use. I refused to put a pen to paper on my own thoughts. I remember giving this method a try just because my favorite soccer player did it. The first thing I wrote down was, "I don't care." It is funny because by the end, the last page of the book had a bunch of soccer drills written down that I was able to do in my backyard. So not only was the journal completely full, but I also actually learned quite a lot and came out a better person and a better soccer player just because I carried around a pen and a journal. Your thoughts shouldn't stay locked up. Write them down and become aware.

43. Never settle.

In school, in soccer, and in life, never settle for less than you deserve. Too many people in this world are wasting their time and effort in jobs or relationships that they are way too good for. Opportunities come and go, so never take the first one that comes your way. Be confident that something better will come along. As long as you are putting forth the effort and improving yourself, then "better" is always just over the horizon. Jumping into scenarios way too soon can lead you to believe that it is the best you can get and there is nothing else out there. Be patient.

In school, don't be average. Go above and beyond and get a 4.0 GPA. Settling for C's and barely scraping by is for the ordinary. Be extraordinary. In soccer, don't settle for a division-3 college offer. Shoot for the stars and fight for a division-1 scholarship. The first offer you get is rarely the best you will receive if you just have patience. And finally in life, don't lower your dreams because you think you aren't good enough. News flash - you are beyond good enough and you just have to keep fighting. Never give up. Never lose hope. Never settle.

Story: I remember receiving my first college letter when I was just a freshman in high school. It was for a division-3 team that was in southeastern Wisconsin. I was completely ecstatic. I was ready to send the coach an email and let him know that I couldn't wait to attend his university in 4 years. My dad thought I was crazy and told me that one day I would be receiving offers from the best division-1 colleges in the country. I didn't believe him. I was ready to settle. But sure enough, a couple years later I was receiving letters from the best college soccer programs in the country. I could have gone to any university I wanted to. And to think, I was going to commit to this little division-3 team in Wisconsin. Time brings opportunity.

44. Don't go searching for love.

You are so young! Love builds over time. So don't waste time trying to create it from nothing right now. Relationships can be fun, but they take away from time that can be spent reaching your dreams. This topic relates back to settling. Don't miss out on your dreams by spending time with someone that you are going to leave once you two head to different colleges and can't take the distance. If a love is meant to be, then it will happen. That once-in-a-lifetime love will come to you, so don't waste time going out and searching for it at an early age. Once you sign that first professional contract, then go ahead and search for your soul mate. But until that time, you need to keep your head on straight.

I am not saying you can't have a boyfriend or girlfriend. I am not saying that relationships are the end to all dreams. I am saying that if you are in a relationship, your partner better add to your improvement and respect your goals. If you are single, then don't spend time searching for "the one." You will have plenty of years down the road to get married. You only have a short time to become a professional soccer player. Once you hit a certain age, you can kiss those dreams goodbye. Love will come to you, but you have to earn your dreams.

Story: I may be a little biased on this topic because I wasted a lot of my high school years with different girlfriends. I thought I had to settle down with a girl and have everything figured out. I could have spent so much more time practicing instead of all the movie dates. I could have bought so much training gear instead of all the dinners. However, if you have a girlfriend or boyfriend now and you are determined that you can reach your dreams with them by your side, then go for it. Prove me wrong. But just make sure they are in the photo of you signing your first contract. Because if they stuck by your side while you fought every day to achieve your dream, then that love is worth it. Don't let it go.

45. Take warm-ups seriously.

Most players think warms-ups are just to get you ready for a game or practice session. They are only partially correct. Warm-ups are also for improvement. Warm-ups are a part of practice, so give it your full attention. Make sure you go through the full routine and work on your form. This will allow you to perform better in the first 10-15 minutes of games. Warm your body up and stretch your muscles. The high intensity warms-ups are always the best.

Another positive from taking warm-ups seriously is the reduction in the amount of injuries that will occur through out your career. Cold muscles don't do well with high activity. You need to invest the time to get your muscles slowly used to quick cuts and fast sprints. The warm-ups are also the first impression that scouts or coaches have of you when they come to your games. Everyone knows how important first impressions are. Show them what you are made of. Stay focused and lead your team. Prepare them for battle.

Story: My first year of professional soccer, I had a teammate who would do his own warm-up on the sideline. He refused to do the warm-ups with the team because he felt they were "insufficient" for him. He felt like he needed his own routine to get ready for games. After only 5 games into the season, he had already suffered 2 muscle injuries. Our trainer obviously knew why this was happening. He approached the player and told him that the only way he would let him play in the games was if he did the warm-ups with the team. He agreed, and he got through the rest of the season without a single injury. This made it clear to me that even though it is "just a warm-up," it is a crucial part to the success of a player, and the success of a team.

46. Avoid laziness and video games.

Laziness should be your worst enemy as a soccer player. To be honest, it's hard not to be lazy with things like Netflix, video games, and donuts. All those things sound so good, but are they worth giving up a dream for? Hell no. It's easier to sit on the couch in front of a TV than play 90 minutes in front of thousands screaming fans. That is why there are more obese people in the world than professional soccer players. It should be an obvious answer when asked which one of those you'd rather be. Laziness is like quick sand, so even one lazy day can get you caught up in a downward spiral.

One of the biggest problems with teenagers these days is video games. There are shooting games, sports games, and fantasy games. Wouldn't you rather be the player that kids choose to play with in FIFA than be the kid sitting on the couch scrolling through which team to pick? Use that as motivation. As your classmates sit there and get excited over a goal scored on the FIFA video game. Be the player in real life that is scoring those goals on the main stage. Make it a goal of yours to be in the FIFA video game.

Story: I went through a video game stage while I was in high school. It was my sophomore year and I had made a friend who was addicted to FIFA. He played it every day like it was his job. We were sitting on the couch one day, playing for 6 hours straight. Once we finished one of our games, he looked over at me and said, "Wouldn't it be cool if one day you were on the game and I could just play with your team?" That was what I needed to get off my ass and get to training. Now, my friend's future goal was in my hands too. Not only would I be a professional soccer player, but also my friend could use me in FIFA to beat all of his records. I was determined.

47. Hold your head high.

Chin up, my friend. The world is yours. Holding your head high at all times is what coaches look for in players. They want to see a player who is ready to take on anything that comes their way with fire in their eyes and in their hearts. Confidence is key for players, and the best way to exhibit that confidence on the outside is to hold your head up high and look ahead. No matter the scenario, stick your chest out and display your pride. Coaches care about how you carry yourself. They notice your body language and how you walk. Make it known that you are fearless and that you own the place.

You can have all the confidence in the world, but if you don't display that confidence, then coaches won't believe in you. Holding your head high on and off the field will be proof of your confidence. When talking to authority, don't look at the ground. When coaches talk to you, keep your chin up and look them in the eyes. Wear your confidence like a cape. Opponents will fear you and teammates will admire you. Just stick your chest out and hold your head high.

Story: Even when I was a confident player, I had a habit of constantly looking at the ground and avoiding eye contact with everyone. I was confident on the inside, but scared out of my mind on the outside. Before a game one day, my teammate couldn't stop talking about this star player the other team had. I looked over at him during warm-ups and he looked like he thought he was God. He stuck his chest out, held his head high, and strutted around the field like it was his. I'll admit I was intimidated. But after scoring a hat trick on his team, I realized that the intimidation was all because of how he carried himself. He glowed with confidence. I immediately wanted to be just like him in that sense. I started to focus more on keeping my chin up and letting my confidence show on the outside. I'm not sure if it has been working, but I like to think that I scare my opponents when I walk onto the field.

48. Know you are the best.

I don't care where you are or who you are playing for. You need to know that, no matter what people say or think, you are the best player on the team. You need to know that you are the best player on the field every time you step foot onto it. The second you think otherwise is the second that you lose all credibility. Treat the field like it is named after you. Know that everyone in the stands is there to watch you. Being the best is a duty that you were made for. Know that you are going to shine on the field and the fans are going to love you. Nobody can touch you. Know that this is the truth.

It may just be a way of thinking, but you need to do it. You need to be able to trust that your abilities are above everyone else around you. Step onto the soccer field, open up your arms, and soak it all in. Walk onto the field with the mindset that you are the greatest thing that has ever happened to this planet. People can call it conceited. They can call it cockiness. But as long as you call it "truth," then their opinions are irrelevant.

Story: This tip is actually some of the best advice I have ever gotten. When my father was my coach, he told me that I needed to believe I am the best player every time I step onto the field. I was hesitant at first, but once I started to believe it on a consistent basis, it was always true. Now, this is the advice I pass on to my younger players. Of course, not every player can be the best on the field, but if they all believe they are the best, then they will succeed. Success isn't always about being the best. Success is about believing you are the best, and backing up your beliefs. Life is too short to lack faith in yourself. Whether practices or games, walk onto the field knowing you are the best player out there.

49. Treat every minute like it is 0-0.

I don't care if your team is winning 10-0. I don't care if your team is losing 10-0. You need to fight like it is 0-0 and the next goal wins. If you can train yourself to think like this, your games will never lack excitement. Coaches absolutely love players who put in all of their effort regardless of scores or conditions. Don't be the player that gives up and asks to get taken off the field when they are losing late in the game. Be the player that picks his or her team up and demands effort. Lead by example and fight for every tackle, every header, and every challenge.

Try and pass this attitude onto your teammates. It is a lot more effective when the whole team believes the game is 0-0 than having just one player out there running like a chicken with its head cut off. A 0-0 game means that every move is crucial. One mistake and you can lose. One goal and your team is in the lead. Have this mentality every second of a 90-minute match and your play will improve. Your body will exert energy that you wouldn't have had otherwise. Push yourself every second of every match, even when victory is unlikely. And never have mercy when your team is winning. Mercy is for the weak.

Story: I had never heard of this technique until I had my first coach who wasn't my dad. In our first game, I scored a quick goal and we were winning 1-0. However, when we lined up for the kick-off, our captain yelled, "0-0, boys!" I was so confused. "Did my goal not count?" I thought to myself. I was mad, so I went chasing after the ball and quickly won it back before scoring again. I was then relieved until again my teammate yelled, "0-0, boys!" I then understood that it was just a team strategy to treat the game like it was tied, no matter what the score was. Ever since that game, I have carried this mentality with me in every game. It clearly works. Just try not to confuse any teammates along the way.

50. Don't be a circus player.

We all know a player who gets the ball and does 4 to 5 step overs in addition to some fancy moves before losing the ball in frustration. Those are the same players that warm-up for games by juggling the ball for a half-hour straight. If you want to know the truth: although that is cool and all, coaches don't care about what you can do in a circus. They care about what you can do in game scenarios. They care about how you are when you take a player 1-on-1 or in front of the goal. Every team has a player who would be better off in the circus than on the soccer field. Don't be that guy.

A coach would much rather see you complete a nice pass than nutmeg a guy and then lose the ball. Dribbling can be affective on the field, but only if there is space allowed. Don't be extravagant if it means you aren't getting things done. Soccer players get paid to win soccer games and do what the coach asks for. Your coach will not ask you to perform tricks out on the field. Focus on the details of real-game situations.

Story: I have never been on a team where the best players on the field were also the best players with tricks. The best players have always seemed to be the ones who had a good touch on the ball and could juggle the ball forever, but never really cared too much for fancy moves. My high school coach always said, "Wow, that's cool. But I think it belongs in the circus, not on the soccer field." That has always made me laugh because it rings so much truth. There is a reason why there are homeless people who do soccer ball tricks on the streets and beg for money. Those skills don't translate to the soccer field. Be careful with how you spend your free time practicing. Prepare yourself for games, not the circus.

51. Improve dribbling first.

However, there is a huge difference between juggling tricks and dribbling skills. Juggling tricks can rarely be used on the soccer field. Those are the moves that deserve to be in the circus. However, dribbling skills are useful on the soccer field. These are the skills that you obtain by setting up cones and making quick cuts and quick touches. More touches in less space are what are going to increase your dribbling ability. Practices should never be dedicated to juggling or doing tricks. Stick to the fundamentals but expand the difficulty.

People will always ask you what your juggling record is, and you should get to the point where you can juggle until your legs get tired. Then, if they ask to see you do some tricks, just laugh and respond with, "I'd rather score goals than do tricks," or "The pay is better for soccer players than for clowns." Question a coach that tells you juggling is more important than dribbling. It is always better to get a thousand touches on the ball dribbling up and down an open field than staying in one place juggling a ball a thousand times.

Story: My youth soccer coach made all of his players learn how to juggle at least 30 times. He gave us this task over summer break and told us that if we couldn't juggle 30 times, that we had to do fitness until we learned to juggle that much. The first day of practice came and the dreaded day was here. Coach blew his whistle and I started to juggle. In the corner of my eye I could see ball after ball hit the ground, as my teammates were quickly defeated. I was the last one standing and stopped only when the coach told me to. My coach was beyond impressed and praised me in front my teammates. He asked me how many hours I put into juggling that summer and I replied, "Maybe 1 or 2 but I mainly just did technical drills." Focus on the skills that matter and the rest will fall into place.

52. Play for fun.

Between the tackles and the hard hits, soccer is actually a really fun and exhilarating sport. No matter your age, you need to understand that people play soccer because it is fun. Forget about money. Forget about trophies. Forget about sponsorship deals. We all started playing this beautiful game as kids because we had fun out there on the field. We need to always remember that kid that we used to be. Remember how happy they were running around on the field. We didn't care if we won or lost. We just wanted to kick a ball around. Times have changed, but don't let your spirit. Always play for fun.

When players who are getting paid millions of dollars stop having fun, their worth begins to drop. You can't be the best possible soccer player if you aren't having fun. When you stop having fun, you subconsciously start putting in less and less effort. Every time you step onto the field, you should be prepared to have the time of your life. If you aren't having fun, maybe soccer isn't your calling. Never forget that soccer is a sport that was made to be fun. Don't stress about contracts or championships. Don't stress at all. Just enjoy it. You are blessed to be able to step on a field and play this beautiful sport.

Story: In my 3rd year as a professional, I started off the season in a slump. The coach was down my throat about scoring and if I didn't start to score soon, he was going to cut me. He was a new coach and so I hadn't really formed a good relationship with him yet. The assistant coach saw how hard he was being on me so before one of the games he came over to me and said, "Just have fun." This advice lifted all the weight off my shoulders, even though my job was on the line. My assistant coach just needed to remind me why I was playing this sport. That was all it took for me to get my game back on track and score some goals. I just needed to have fun again.

53. Shoot the ball!

Never hesitate when you are in front of the goal. I don't care if you are a defender who has never scored a goal in your life. Shoot the ball. Shooting the ball is a sign of confidence that every coach wants to see in a player. It tells a lot about a player when they are right in front of the goal and have a wide-open shot, and decide to pass on the opportunity and give the ball to a teammate. "Shooting the ball" pertains to more than just on the soccer field.

Shoot the ball in all aspects of life. Pull the trigger. Advance your career at every opportunity possible. Take risks that the average person wouldn't usually take. Sign up for a soccer camp across the country. Book a plane ticket to Europe. Email some agencies. Don't be scared. Fear will hold you back from your dreams. Fear will hold you back from scoring goals and winning games. So shoot the ball and don't second-guess it.

Story: When I was about 8-years-old, my team had an indoor game. The game was tied and I was running up the sideline with the ball at my feet. I ran right in front of our team's bench when my dad yelled, "You take that ball and you put it in that goal." It was such an obvious statement, but it worked. I took the ball up the field and I shot it into the back of the net. I have used that moment through out my life to make a lot of key decisions. Whenever I need to make a crucial decision in my life, I think to myself, "What is the obvious choice that is going to get me closer to my dreams." I drop all fear. I put aside any unnecessary factors. And I shoot the ball. My dad taught me to always take risks. What is the worst that will happen? Either you miss the shot, or you get all of the glory... Take the shot.

54. Win the ball back!

Watch a game of soccer and calculate the number of players who immediately win the ball back after losing it. The number is usually very small. Put yourself in the minority and make it a point to always win the ball back right away. Of course, you don't want to lose the ball in the first place. But once you do, pressure the ball as closely as you can until you make a tackle. Nothing is worse than seeing a player lose the ball and just walk back on defense. Those players just assume one of their teammates is going to fight to win the ball back. You know what those players are called: lazy.

This is one of the make-or-break moments in a game for a scout. Every scout knows that you are going to lose the ball at least once a game. If you didn't, then they would have signed you up by now. But the scout isn't looking to see how you lose the ball. They are looking at how you react once you have lost it. One second of hesitation can decide whether or not you win the ball back. You need to train yourself to react immediately to win the ball back. Don't complain about losing the ball or yell at a teammate for not getting open. Get that ball!

Story: In college, I remember playing really badly one game. I couldn't score if my life depended on it. I was missing shots and losing the ball and I was so frustrated with myself. After the game, I remember making eye contact with our head coach as he was walking in my direction. I knew he was about to yell at me and make me look stupid. I had just played the worst game of my life. But instead, he complimented me as he gave me a pat on the back. He said, "I loved your fighting spirit this game. We need more of that from you." I knew this was targeted at my effort to win the ball back after I had lost it so many times. I wasn't as disappointed in myself anymore because I did really work my ass off. I was proud. But then the coach walked away and under his breath he said, "We could use some f***ing goals too, though."

55. Never create back-up plans.

Will Smith said, "There's no reason to have a plan B, because it distracts from plan A." I could not agree more with this statement. If you truly want to become a professional soccer player, make that your plan A, plan B, and plan C. Make that your only plan. If you don't make it, then come up with another plan later on. But I guarantee if you put in the work, your dreams will become a reality. You don't need distractions in your life. If you split time between chasing dreams, then you won't achieve either. You need to make your decision and stick to it. There will be setbacks, but stick to the plan.

You will have people in your life that will ask, "But what if it doesn't work out." Those people aren't worth talking to. Surround yourself with people who know that it will work out. Back-up plans are for people who have doubt. If you doubt yourself, then maybe you should have a plan B. If you doubt yourself, then maybe you aren't cut out to be a pro soccer player. Always believe that your plan A will fall into place. You are going to do whatever it takes to make it happen, so don't expect to fail.

Story: I never had a back-up plan. My parents always wanted me to go to school and get my degree. They told me that I couldn't play soccer forever, and they were right. But I couldn't worry about life after soccer until soccer was out of my life. I put all of my focus and effort into soccer because that was my only dream. If I had spent more time in college learning about business, then I would have spent less time on the field putting my work in. I was determined to play professional soccer. I could always get my degree after my soccer career. Things worked out perfectly, because I committed myself to my plan A without even considering a plan B.

56. Don't force things.

Soccer calls for a lot of patience. If you don't have patience, then you won't make it as a professional soccer player. You have to be able to wait for the right opportunities or openings on the field. If you dribble up the field and pick your head up, you have 12 options. You can pass it to any 10 of your teams, you can shoot, or you can dribble into space. Now remember not every teammate will be open. You won't always be close to goal. And you may not always have space. You have to be able to, in a split second, figure out the best choice of play. Always pick the safe bet when in doubt.

Aside from being in the final third, passing may be your best bet. Don't always feel the pressure to get into the final third. It is okay to go backwards. Coaches would rather you play a ball back to your goalkeeper than try and force a ball to the target and lose the ball. Always choose "ease" before "please," unless you are close to goal. Have patience. Sometimes, things just aren't meant to be. Don't force them to fall into place. On or off the field, it is important to know when things just aren't going to work out. Don't force things.

Story: In my senior year of high school, every team we played was putting two or three players on me to make sure I never got the ball. Even as defenders surrounded me, my teammates were still trying to get me the ball because I was the goal-scorer. A couple games into the season, our coach said, "No more trying to get James the ball. He is now our decoy." I was a little upset. But I also knew this was necessary for us to win. So every game, I stayed out wide, dragging a few defenders with me. My teammates were no longer trying to force me the ball, because they now had a lot more options without me clogging up the middle. Always choose to play simple in the build up. But when you get close to goal, go for the spectacular.

57. Protect your teammates.

Teammates are family. I don't care if you fight a lot. I don't care if one of them stole your ex. You need to treat them like siblings. Don't ever let someone disrespect or hurt your teammates. You need to be willing to stand up for each and every one of them. You need to be ready to jump in front of a punch for them. As a team member, and especially as a team leader, it is your job to protect your teammates and keep them out of harm. Protecting your teammates also means protecting them from stupidity. If you see a teammate making a lot of stupid tackles, pull them aside and calm them down. Do whatever it takes to keep your teammates in the right mindset.

When you protect your teammates, your team will succeed. You will build positive relationships and trust will grow within the team. When you have people's backs, they begin to have yours. Successful teams need to be an indestructible unit. Coaches admire leaders who can stand up for their teammates and make sure they are safe. If someone makes an unfair tackle on your teammate, let him or her know how you feel. Do it respectfully of course, but use some authority.

Story: The first team captain I had as a professional didn't really like me. I'm not sure if it was because I was young, or if it was because I was American. I just remember that in the middle of the season, I received a hard tackle from behind. As I began to get up off the ground, I saw our captain come sprinting over and shove the defender to the ground. I was shocked at first. Then I realized how devoted this guy was to protecting his teammates and I was overcome with respect for him. I thought he had completely hated me until that moment. Well, maybe he still did. But he made sure that no one messed with me. Now I make sure that I am that type of leader. No one messes with my teammates. My teammates are my family.

58. Go out, but set a curfew.

It is okay to have some fun every once in a while and hang out with your friends away from soccer. Soccer isn't meant to tear you apart and burn you out. Every now and then you can go out and enjoy your time responsibly. When you have these "soccer-free" nights, set a curfew and stick to it. Getting to bed at a reasonable time will allow you to still wake up early the next day and get to work. If you stay out too late, then you won't be in the proper mindset the following day to work towards your goal. You don't want to lose a night to friends, and also lose the whole next day trying to recover from lack of sleep.

Setting a curfew will also give you a reason to leave at a specific time. If your friends try to get you to stay, you can tell them your parents set a strict curfew. You are still able to have a good time and connect with friends. Trust me, nothing that important is going to happen after 9 or 10 PM. Enjoy the night and get excited to get back to the grind the following day. Every high school student needs to have a social life, so don't let soccer ruin that. But also try not to consider yourself in the same category as "every high school student."

Story: I had a close group of friends toward the end of high school that was hanging out every weekend. They were fun to be around and always made me laugh. I was happy when I was with them. I wanted to hang out with them but I also didn't want to take too much time away from chasing my dreams. I allowed myself to hang out with them twice a month, but I made sure I earned it. If I felt I performed poorly in the days leading up to the "hang out day", I would make up a reason why I couldn't hang out with them. And I always had a curfew. This way, I was able to enjoy my time with them, but I also made it clear to them and to myself that soccer was my true happiness.

59. Take school seriously.

High school is probably the first time that you have ever truly been academically challenged in your lifetime. Every class before this has been an "automatic pass." You've never really had to try. You need to treat school as a stepping-stone for your career. The better you do in school, the better the college you will get into. Also, the better you do in school, the smarter you will become in social situations. Treat school like it is part of your soccer career. It affects your opportunities more than you think.

College coaches love recruiting smart kids, because that means they can use academic scholarships to bring you in. They don't have to use only athletic scholarships to try and persuade you to attend their university. Coaches also love smart soccer players because it shows that they are intelligent on and off the field. Coaches love players that have a good head on their shoulders. Your grades in high school also provide coaches with a good preview of how you will perform in college. Coaches want players who can raise their team's average GPA and give their program a good reputation.

Story: I was not a fan of school. I absolutely hated it, but I knew I had to do well if I wanted to get into a top division-1 program. I set aside an hour or two after school to talk with teachers and get all of the help I could get. I wasn't the smartest kid, but I put in the work necessary to get a solid GPA. Then, when it was time to take the ACT, I studied for hours and hours. Top universities were telling me certain scores and cumulative GPA's that I needed to get in order to receive academic scholarships. I typed up those requirements and printed them out. I taped them on my bedroom door and made sure that I worked my ass off to get them. Make sure you take school seriously. Soccer may be your life, but school can still help you achieve success.

60. Find a stress-reliever off the field.

Playing soccer all day every day sounds fun, but it can be stressful at times. Every soccer player needs to find a way to relieve stress when they step off the soccer field. Some players do yoga. Some players meditate. Some players even just go for walks. Search for a stress-relieving hobby and don't be afraid to use it. We all need an escape at times. It is important to have a strategy to unwind and let go of anything that is bringing negativity into your life. It is good to clear your mind at times. A soccer career can be overwhelming.

Stress can drive teenagers into depression or anxiety, and you are not immune. No matter how strong you think you are, it is always possible to get burnt out by overworking yourself. You have a long and successful road ahead of you, so don't be afraid to take short breaks to catch your breath and relieve stress. Soccer brings joy 99% of the time, but you need to be prepared for the other 1%. Find something or someone that makes you happy and relieves your stress. Stress can get in the way of success. Don't let it get in the way of yours.

Story: I had reached my breaking point in my junior year of high school. I had enough of soccer because I felt so much pressure and I had nowhere to turn. Then one day, I walked over to the local soccer fields down the road from my house. I put in my ear buds, turned on some chill music, and just walked. I cleared my mind and suddenly I felt so light. The world seemed so simple and my stress had disappeared. I went home feeling refreshed. From that point forward, whenever I felt burnt out or overwhelmed, I just went down to the local park and walked. It doesn't seem like much, but it kept me in the right mindset. It cleared my head of all negativity. I strongly encourage you to find your stress-reliever and use it frequently.

61. Learn to pump yourself up.

There will not always be motivation around you. You will not always be put in the best scenarios to be inspired. You need to learn how to find motivation from nothing, and drive yourself into a successful position. You may find yourself in a game with no meaning, or a practice with many players absent. It is a moment like that where you need to push yourself to still fight your heart out and improve your game. Pump up music won't always be available. Championships aren't always on the line. Be able to look yourself in the mirror and tell yourself, "My performance today matters."

Some days, you may just not feel it. You may wake up on a rainy Saturday and think that today may just need to be a rest day. How do you react in moments like this? Adapt yourself to getting motivated even in the moments of despair. Create a routine for yourself, even if it just a quick 10-second affirmation. Learn to get yourself pumped up, even for the little things. Get excited for life. Get excited to live another day in the life of a dream chaser. Getting pumped up may seem impossible some days. Push through it and remember that every second is an opportunity to improve.

Story: When I first arrived in Europe, I was living in a small apartment in the middle of nowhere. I had no friends. I barely had any money. Finding motivation was nearly impossible. No one was waking me up in the morning telling me to get my ass out of bed. I had to set an alarm early every morning and convince myself that going for a run was necessary for my success. I had to push myself every second of every day, even though I only had practice for 2 hours. When I found myself feeling lazy, I looked in the mirror and said out loud, "There are other players out there in the world that are trying to be better than me." I couldn't let that happen. Even on my off days, I needed to be inspired. Otherwise, those other players would beat me to my dreams.

62. Accept injuries and move forward.

Small or big, injuries are bound to happen. Whether it is a sprained ankle or a concussion, it will happen to you at least once in your career. When these setbacks occur, you can't take it as a sign from God to end your career. You can't take it as a sign to take a break. You need to understand that these things happen. The best way to bounce back is to work 1-on-1 with a trainer and come back even stronger. There are specific ways to recover the right way for every injury. There are stretches and exercises that benefit every muscle, ligament, or bone injury. If you don't have a trainer, then Google ways to recover from whatever injury it is.

Sometimes, injuries affect you more mentally than physically. Having mental setbacks are way worse than any physical setback. Gaining back confidence and belief in yourself is always tricky after having to sit out a couple games or practices. The past is the past and you need to remember the bigger dream here. The dream isn't to go through your career injury-free. Your dream is to become a professional soccer player. No injury is big enough to hold you back from those dreams. You can bounce back from anything. Accept the injuries, big or small, and move forward.

Story: After my first ACL repair surgery, I was ready to give up. I didn't think I could ever come back from such an ugly injury. Mentally, I was broken. But then I went to practice and talked to one of my teammates who had a similar injury before. He didn't have just one ACL injury. He had 3 of them. I was so shocked because he was one of the best players on our team even after having 3 surgeries on the same injury. He told me, "If you truly believe in yourself, you could have both legs amputated and still be a soccer star." He said it with such confidence that I knew he had to be right. I came back from my injury stronger and better than ever.

63. Take advantage of opportunities.

Opportunities are few and far between in the world, especially for someone who has such an extreme dream. You need to be able to create opportunities for yourself, as well as know when you have the right opportunity right in front of you. Being aware of beneficial situations will propel you into the proper steps on the journey to the ultimate goal. You should never jump at the first opportunity you receive, because experience will be key to knowing which opportunities are the right ones for you.

When you see the right opportunity, jump at it with everything you've got. Constantly look at ways that you can build your career. Study the game and be on the lookout for key injuries or player releases on professional teams. The soccer economy consists of a lot of supply but not so much demand. When the demand is there, be the supply worth demanding. You need to be persistent with your approach. Push yourself into positive positions. See opportunities as breakaways. If you have the chance, you better score. If you don't score, you may not get that open for a breakaway for the rest of the game. Put away your chances, on and off the field.

Story: When I was coming back from my second big injury, I was constantly on the Internet looking to see if any key players had gotten injured in Europe. I didn't take my eyes off the news in several different countries. I was determined that my dreams were not over. All I needed was the right opportunity and I knew I could come back and be better than ever. Sure enough, a striker got injured and I flew over to Europe to try and take his spot. I was offered a new contract and I was happier than ever. Opportunities don't happen very often. And the right opportunities are even more rare. Stay on your toes and be ready to take advantage of your opportunities.

64. Pick placement over power.

This is one of the fundamental tips that you always received from your youth soccer coach. Even in the pros, you start to realize that this advice almost always remains to stay true. When you get yourself in front of the goal, don't panic. Panicking is the worst thing you can do as a goal-scorer. It usually leads to a frantic swing at the ball with all of your might. You can ask any goalkeeper and I guarantee they would rather have a strong shot fired right at them than a slow shot that is placed perfectly in the corner. Make the goalkeeper work. Most powerful shots end up going over the goals anyways. It is hard to keep these kinds of strikes under control.

The best goal-scorers are able to pick out even the slightest opening and take advantage of it. The best way to improve this sector of your game is to practice. Shoot, shoot, and shoot some more. Go to the closest field and bring as many balls as you have. Don't practice firing the ball as hard as you can. The strength in your shots will come from the weight training you do. Spend your technical practices working on your placement. It is hard to teach players placement shots, so coaches love when there is a player who stays calm and passes the ball into the corner of the net. Be patient and don't panic. Just score.

Story: When I was a youth soccer player, I would always shoot the ball with all of my power. I could be inside the box and still feel the need to fire the ball as hard as I could. I didn't understand why I couldn't score. Then, I started to watch more and more soccer and slowly started to realize that most goals are scored by taking it easy and focusing on placement. I have learned that even shots from beyond 25 yards out are more successful when you just pick a corner and hit it.

65. Play pick-up games.

Not all of your practice needs to happen in a professional setting. The best sessions I have gone through have been pick-up games or sessions with my friends. Whenever you are asked to participate in a pick-up game, take advantage of it. Pick-up games may be poorly organized, but they are always a solid opportunity to improve your abilities and get in-game action. Practicing on your own is good for your technical ability, but taking on defenders and having high pressure will always be better to prepare you for the next level.

If pick-up games aren't a thing where you are from, make them a thing. Call your friends up or get your team together. Take initiative to set something up that will allow you to get a game going. Even if it is 2-on-2, it is worth it. Pick-up games allow you to practice skills that you wouldn't be able to work on in practice or games when your coach is watching. Approach every pick-up game with the attitude of winning. Focus on improving your game and advancing your skills. Be the player that is always picked first. Play to win.

Story: When I was 12, I went on a trip to Spain with an all-star team. We traveled around Spain and played against other youth teams. The competition was all right, but then we went home to our hotel every night and the real competition began. I, along with a couple of my teammates, would go out to the back alley and play with a couple of the local kids who were always out there. These players were always way better than the competition we faced in the actual games. This is how it is in Spain, Brazil, and many other countries. Players form their skills by playing street ball and pick-up games. Not everyone can afford organized sports. And to be honest, I feel that playing on concrete in small areas works a lot more on footwork than playing on a big field with 20 field players. Take advantage of pick-up games. Always be looking to improve your in-game abilities.

66. Be a perfectionist.

Chase perfection until the day you die. On the field, in the classroom, in the office, be perfect. It is rare that you will find yourself making zero mistakes. However, if you are on a constant search for perfection, your mistakes will become fewer and fewer. As you go through life, always look to make things a little better. Improve your workplace. Improve your teammates. Improve your homework. Adjust things if they don't look right. Tell someone if they are doing something wrong. Taking this initiative in life will transition onto the soccer field. Perfectionists can be annoying, but they are usually the ones who become successful.

Being a perfectionist isn't easy. Trying to chase perfection can be frustrating, because you will never actually be truly perfect. But you can get extremely close to it. Work on completing every pass without a single errant one. Try and get every shot on target. Better yet, try and score every shot you take in a game. Measure your growth and see how much you improve just by trying to be perfect. If you focus your whole life on chasing perfection, then chasing your dreams won't be a problem.

Story: I once had a girlfriend who was a perfectionist. It was one of the most annoying things in the world. But if I said it didn't help me improve, then I would be lying. She always made sure everything around her was in place. Before I knew it, I slowly started to become like her. On and off the field, I started looking around myself and wondering how I could make things better. I would fix my socks to be the same level at knee-height. I would be mad at myself if a single pass I made was just an inch or so off. I started focusing more on shooting the ball as close to the post as possible. Being a perfectionist is a hard thing to do, considering you will never truly achieve perfection. But in the process of chasing it, you will slowly start to see yourself grow into a better soccer player and even a better person.

67. Always think one step ahead.

Be futuristic, but don't always look deep into the future. Sometimes, you are best off just thinking a few seconds ahead. Being able to look around you and analyze situations is an amazing trait to have as a soccer player. Players need to be able to predict what the opposition is going to do. This trait takes a lot of studying. You acquire this knowledge by watching soccer and observing the movements of the players. You aren't just a soccer player. You are also a soccer analyst. You need to understand the game to the point where you can predict one step ahead at all times.

Always know what you are going to do next. Expect the ball at any and every second, even if you are on the opposite side of the field. Staying on your toes will prepare you for what is going to happen next. Understanding what is going on around you is key. But knowing what you are going to do with it all is even more important. Always allow yourself 3 options at all times. Look around you and analyze the 3 best options at every moment in a game. Get in the habit of being on a constant lookout for better options. Never get caught in the moment unprepared. There are two types of players: the players that receive the ball, look up, and decide what to do, and the players who have already decided what they are going to do before they even get the ball. Be the latter.

Story: I started to quiz myself when I watch soccer games. I turn on a game on TV and I grab the remote. I pause the game every 2-3 minutes and analyze what will happen next. If I am right with how the next moves unravel, whether it's a decision or a certain pass, I subtract a minute from fitness training. This way, I work on improving my analysis of game situations and I reward myself for being correct. Create incentives for yourself and you will enjoy learning a lot more.

68. Find every inch of space.

Off the soccer field, this advice can be used as a metaphor for always looking for ways to improve. There are always options out there for you to take advantage of. You just need to find them. The world is filled with adventures and lessons, and you need to put yourself out in the world and express yourself. You need to understand yourself and see how the world can help you grow and improve. Find every trait that you can improve and even the traits that you don't have yet. Find every connection, every lesson, every drill, and use it to expand your horizons.

On the field, literally find every single open inch of space and expose it. Players should look like ants to you on a soccer field. You need to be attracted to the green space and head in that direction. Open up the field. When you are dribbling up the field, seek every open area that you can head to, and then make your best decision. The space around you is plentiful; you just need to find it. The world is your soccer field, don't be afraid to travel and create a diverse opposition for yourself. You will improve your awareness. Life will fall into place for you as long as you are constantly looking for growth. Find the space and explore it.

Story: Growing up, I always had one thing in mind when I was on the soccer field: find the goal. I could be at midfield and my only focus would be to find the goal and shoot. Nothing else mattered to me. I started to struggle when I was far from goal, and I needed to change my mentality. Then, I started to just look for space. With or without the ball, I would look around myself and try to find space that I could expose. As my team possessed the ball, I would get the ball and look for space. Then I would again get the ball back and look for space. If I did this enough times, soon enough I would be close to the goal and I could score. Looking for space will slowly but surely head you in the right direction. Don't always look so far ahead. Just focus on finding every inch of space accessible to you.

69. Use every inch of space.

Finding the space is half the battle. But once you find it, use it to your advantage. When you are on the soccer field, tiptoe the sidelines. When you see space behind the defense, expose it and create a goal-scoring opportunity. Space is all around you, but only the best soccer players can find it and use it as a benefit. Life is filled with opportunities. But if you don't use them, then they might as well have never been offered. One of the best speeches ever given was on the movie "Every Given Sunday."

"You know, when you get old in life things get taken from you. That's part of life. But, you only learn that when you start losing stuff. You find out that life is just a game of inches. So is football. Because in either game, life or football, the margin for error is so small. I mean, one half step too late or too early, you don't quite make it. One half step too late or too early, you don't quite catch it. The inches we need are everywhere around us. They are in every break of the game, every minute, every second. On this team, we fight for that inch. On this team, we tear ourselves, and everyone around us to pieces, for that inch. We claw with your fingernails for that inch. Because we know, when we add up all those inches, that's going to make the f***ing difference between winning and losing, between living and dying. I'll tell you this. In any fight, it is the guy who is willing to die, who is going to win that inch. And I know, if I am going to have any life anymore, it is because I am still willing to fight and die for that inch, because that is what living is."

Story: I watched that speech every day for a whole year. Now, I don't hesitate to win every inch possible, in life and on the soccer field. I put my body on the line every opportunity possible to gain an inch on my opponent. My best advice for you is to do the same. Every inch can be the difference between a win and a loss.

70. Want to take every set piece.

You can claim that you are confident. But if you don't play confidently on the soccer field, then all that confidence goes to waste. When the time comes to be a clutch player, take that step. Life is too short not to step up to the plate when your team needs you. Be the player that proves your confidence game in and game out, no matter how well you are doing. Never let anyone push you around. You need to know that your team is looking at you to lead them to victory. Carry around so much confidence that it spreads to, not just your teammates, but also everyone you come in contact with in life.

Coaches and scouts want to recruit players who are confident to have the ball at their feet. They want to have players on their team that don't shy away from a penalty or free kick. Picture every free kick or penalty as a chance to score. A penalty may be the only shot on goal that you get all game. Don't be scared. Know that you are going to put the ball in the back of the net. Be the hero. Your team needs you.

Story: I have never passed on a penalty or free kick. Penalties should be automatic goals. Who would want to pass up an automatic goal? And when it comes to free kicks, stick to the "placement over power" strategy. Just hit the target. Every time you have an open shot on goal, especially with the closest defender beyond 8 yards away, take it. Only players who don't have confidence in their abilities will pass up on a penalty or free kick. Coaches don't want to put someone on their team who doesn't believe in themselves. Whenever I take a penalty or free kick, I take a deep breath. I forget about the world. I ignore the defenders. I ignore the fans. All I can see is the goal and the goalkeeper. And the goalkeeper never has a chance

71. Train both feet.

Believe it or not, this causes a lot of trouble for players, even at the collegiate level. Coaches get extremely frustrated when they witness a player have the ball on their weak side with a wide-open shot on goal and decide to cut the ball back to their strong side. By the time you manage to get the ball on your strong foot, your opportunity has passed and the defense has recovered. Build your weak foot up so that it isn't your weak foot anymore. Be just as confident on your weak side as on your strong side. The game of soccer will come much easier to you when you don't have to constantly have the ball on one side of your body.

Adding this dimension to your game will double the amount of opportunities in the future. If you are only good with your right foot, then chances are coaches will recruit you to play on the right side. If you are only good with your left foot, then coaches will only put you on the left side. Being confident with both feet opens up all positions as good spots for you to fit in. Have daily sessions where you imitate your strong foot by using your weak foot. You can go as slow as you want. Practice your shooting, passing, and dribbling. Have patience. It'll be worth it.

Story: When I was 8-years-old, I was told that I didn't have a left foot. I couldn't disagree. I only ever used my right foot, even if the ball was on my left side. To be honest, I was scared to use my left foot because I knew it wasn't very good. I was watching soccer with my dad one day and he pointed out, "Look at how good these players are with both of their feet." I wanted to be a professional soccer player at that point, and I knew that I wouldn't make it if my left foot sucked. I spent the whole next season only practicing with my left foot. I wouldn't let myself use my right foot. No matter the case, I used my left foot. At first, it was awful. But by the end of the season, my left foot was better than my right foot. I am sure glad I spent that year wisely. I have played 5 years professionally on the left wing.

72. Speed train as much as possible.

Life as a soccer player will be hard as hell if you are slow. Choose to be a cheetah over a turtle. The whole tortoise and the hare story means nothing in a 90-minute soccer match. Bust your ass and move those feet. People may think that slowness can't be cured. They are lying. If you do have heavy feet, there are always speed camps available. If you can't find any, YouTube won't let you down. Invest your money in a speed ladder or some hurdles. Treat yourself to a running parachute. If you put in the work, you will slowly start to improve your pace. I strongly believe that nothing is more important in the game of soccer than speed.

Speed is one of the first things that usually catches a scout's eye when he or she is watching a game. If you want to stand out, be the fastest player on the field. Every day should consist of some type of speed training session. If you consistently train your quick muscles to fire, they will adjust. Add resistance to your training. Add weights. Add obstacles to increase your quickness. Speed is an attribute that every player and team needs. Even if you have zero technical ability, your speed could still help you get places. Wake up every morning faster than you were the day before.

Story: At an early age, I knew that I needed to be fast if I wanted to reach my dreams. I was willing to do whatever it took to always be the fastest player on the field. I bought medicine balls, resistance bands, speed parachutes, speed ladders, cones, hurdles, and everything in between. Our garage was filled with this training equipment. I may have pissed off my parents but I don't regret a single thing. I have never been on the field with someone faster than me. I put in the work. You should too.

73. Forget negativity.

Never allow a negative thought to cross your mind. The biggest turn off for a coach is when he or she hears a potential recruit yell something negative at a coach, teammate, or referee. Possess nothing but positivity. Negativity attracts negativity. It doesn't matter if you are struggling or if you are going through a rough patch. You need to be the most positive person in the world once you step onto the field. Even off the field, it is crucial to only allow positivity into your life. You need to form a negativity shield that keeps out negative people, negative influences, negative thoughts, and negative feelings. Life is good. You are able to chase your dreams. There is no room for negativity in your life.

Coaches can tell when you have negativity on your mind. It carries a stench that can't be shaken. Your body language is affected. Your attitude shifts. Your decisions on the field are altered. A positive player is a prosperous player. If you feel that one of your teammates is being too negative, cheer them up. Being a leader consists of many different small jobs and being a therapist is one of them. Once you have conquered your own mindset, spread the positivity onto your teammates.

Story: I have a very precise routine that I go through when a negative thought crosses my mind. First, I take a deep breath. Then, I count to 3. As I finish, I remember back to the moment when I signed my first professional contract. That moment conquers all others. I am automatically consumed by positivity and I forget what the negative thought even was. Find a moment in your life that brought you nothing but pure bliss. Flashback to that point in time every time your mood swings the wrong way. You need to remember that you are blessed. You don't deserve any kind of negativity in your life.

74. Leave personal life off the field.

It doesn't matter if the girl of your dreams just dumped you or if your pet is sick. Once you step onto the field, nothing else matters. The field is your sanctuary and it needs to be treated as such. Don't think about your homework. Don't think about your significant other. Don't think about your friend's drama. Focus on scoring goals, embarrassing defenders, leading your team, and winning soccer games. Everything else is irrelevant. If you plan on making soccer your career, then it deserves your full attention. Your opponents aren't busy worrying about how your pet dog is doing at home without you, so why should you? Your personal life can wait for the next 90 minutes.

As a teenager, your personal life is filled with drama and discontent. But soccer should relieve all of those negative thoughts in your mind. The soccer field should be considered your happy place. Coaches can usually tell when a player is having trouble off the field by the way they carry themselves on the field. This can fall into the category of "forget any negativity." But you should also put aside any positive things going on in your personal life. You just had your first kiss? Congratulations. But you have a soccer game to win, so clear your mind and focus on kicking some ass.

Story: My junior year of high school was a record-breaking year for me. However, it could have been a lot better if I didn't have a girlfriend. There was nothing wrong with my relationship. I was happy. But I was as distracted as ever. I would step onto the field and spend most of the game looking for my girlfriend in the stands. I would try and make her laugh. I made funny faces at her. The whole game I was just worried about what was going on with her and what she was thinking. I could've done so much better that year. I could have scored so many more goals if I had just built a wall around the field and shut out my personal life for 90 minutes. Learn from my mistakes.

75. Apply for better jobs.

This advice should follow you through out your whole life. Applying for jobs that you think you can get will probably land you a job. But is that the best you can do? Apply for jobs that you don't think you will get. You'll never know if you don't try. Take a chance and apply for the top jobs in your field. Ask for tryouts with the top clubs in Europe. Send your transcripts to the best colleges in America. You may not always get accepted or get offered a contract. But one of these times, you will surprise yourself. Believe in yourself and set your standards high. You can't go through life settling because you felt that you weren't good enough.

Put yourself in a position where you aren't the best applicant. Surround yourself with applicants or trialists that have better skills than you. Being in those kinds of groups will make you better. You will learn from those experiences. Coaches don't always search the world for the best players. Sometimes, they wait for players to come to them and prove that they want to be a part of the team. Take a risk. Take a million risks. Don't doubt yourself. Although you won't succeed every time, all you need is one chance and your career can take off.

Story: I enjoy sending my résumé to top businesses because I respect their feedback. I have always received honest feedback when I got turned down by some of the top companies in the country. Feedback is a necessity if you want to improve your skills. I have learned so much about myself by listening to their opinions. If I could go back in time, I would have sent my résumé and videos to coaches all around Europe. And instead of just accepting the rejections I received, I would have asked for their honest thoughts and opinions. I may not have gotten a tryout, but I would learn. And as I slowly improved, one of those times an opportunity would arise. Keep trying. Never doubt your abilities and never set limits for yourself.

76. Empty your gas tank.

This advice works for leaving everything you have on the field. Every game and every practice, put every bit of effort you have left into it. Never leave the field with any energy left. You should be ready to fall to your knees in exhaustion. But this advice is actually meant for life. Every day is a fresh start, so why not make the most of it? Every night as you go to bed, ask yourself, "Did I really give today my all?" If you answer "yes" to this question, then you are doing it right. If you feel that you could still give more, then don't go to bed yet. Your day isn't over yet. You shouldn't just "go" to bed every night. You should "collapse" into bed every night. Empty your gas tank every day you are alive.

Improvement doesn't come easily. It happens when you are constantly extending your limits further and further from where you are. You should act like a magnet with the same charge as your limits. The better you get, the further away from you your limits fade. Pushing yourself to your fullest potential every day is a way to escape all limits. Your body adjusts to the work you put it through. Emptying your gas tank may suck at first. But stick to it. You can't let one drop of energy go unused.

Story: In high school, I looked at myself in the mirror every night before I went to bed. When I asked myself if I really gave my all, a lot of times my answer was, "No, but I'm tired." This type of attitude made me miss out on a lot of potential improvement. Once reality hit me, I knew that I had to change my mentality. I was tired mentally, but physically I could give more. I started to go back outside and train some more when I felt that I hadn't given enough energy for the day. I knew that emptying my gas tank on a daily basis was the only way I could get to my dreams. If you are going to live life right, live it to the fullest. Push yourself.

77. Have a game day routine.

Consistency, consistency, consistency. Coaches love to see a player that approaches every game the same way no matter what. They love to see players that can consistently compete at the highest level and always be the best player on the team. The best way to do this is to create a daily routine that you follow on every game day. A consistent routine will train your body and get it ready for games. Your body is able to adapt to the certain foods or motions it goes through. Following the same routine on game day will tell your body that a 90-minute high-intensity workout is about to occur. This way, your muscles always feel loose and ready, and your body is ready for action.

Daily routines need to fit into your daily life, and shouldn't be anything too extraordinary. You can't be a vegetarian every other day, but then eat 5 pounds of bacon on game day to prepare you for your victory. Don't be too extraordinary. Consistency is what we are looking for here. Figure out a prime time to always wake up at. Plan out your meals to always be scheduled at the same time. Plan pre-game workouts and activities that remain constant. No matter what, always stick to this routine on game days. If you manage to mess it up even just once, it will get to your head and your game may suffer. Create a trustworthy routine and follow it strictly.

Story: My game day routine always starts at 9:00 AM. I allow myself to sleep in a little longer than usual because I need to be well rested. I eat 4 pieces of bacon and 3 scrambled eggs. I go for a half-hour walk. Then, I go on YouTube and watch goal highlights. I eat pasta for lunch and mentally prepare myself for the game. It is hard when game times change. But as long as your day remains the same beside the time of the game, then you should be just fine. Remember: consistency, consistency, consistency.

78. Never forget the fundamentals.

Remember what you learned in your first year of soccer. Remember what you learned in first grade. Remember what you learned in your first try-out. Remember all of it. I promise you, you will never want to forget it. Even though going over fundamentals can be boring, you need to do it. It may seem like a waste of time, but it is still improving your game. You still need to practice them every day.

Fundamentals are taught at such a young age because they are necessary at all levels of the game. They are called "fundamentals" for a reason. They are always present. They are the keys to the game and knowing how to play it. Run up and down the field touching the ball with your laces, the inside of your foot, and the outside of your foot. When you have shooting practice, still focus on keeping your knee over the ball, striking it with your laces, and leaning forward. It is absolutely insane the amount of times you will see poor fundamentals, even in a professional game. Coaches don't want a player that can't keep the ball under a crossbar. They don't want players who think it is okay to use their toe to pass the ball to a teammate. The fundamentals are often forgotten. And practicing the fundamentals will improve all aspects of your game. It may not seem complicated or complex, but it works with your brain to make those moves second nature.

Story: I once played against an opponent, professionally, who just couldn't hit the target. He had many opportunities, but every shot he took went over the bar. He would strike the ball on a breakaway and it would go 10 yards too high. His coach had enough and yelled, "Lean forward when you shoot it!" I chuckled to myself because this advice was so simple, yet it seemed as though the player had forgotten it completely since he was a kid. He obviously listened to his coach, because he leaned forward the next shot he had. He was finally able to keep his shot on the ground. It went wide, though…

79. Make money and reinvest it.

As a teenager, chances are you are going to need to introduce yourself into the job field. Your parents may force you to find a job. To be honest though, getting a job at an early age will benefit you a lot in the future. You will learn discipline, respect, and responsibility. Even better, you'll have that cash flow. View every dollar as an opportunity. They are opportunities for you to grow your soccer skills and your chances of reaching your dreams. Making money is important because the sooner you make it, the sooner you can reinvest it in yourself.

Invest your money towards your goals. Buy things that help you achieve your dreams. Buy training gear. Buy private lessons with a coach. Put yourself in soccer camps. Buy educational DVDs. Buy soccer coaching books. The more money you have, the more resources you can provide yourself for your improvement. Not everyone in the world is as blessed as you are. Some players need to improve themselves with a ball and an open field of sand. Yet they still have the dedication to make it to the pros. So, what's your excuse? Don't put your money into video games or fast food. Put your money where it is going to benefit you the most. Put it into your development.

Story: My first actual job was working in a factory, inspecting car parts. It wasn't too difficult, but it made a decent paycheck, especially as a kid. I remember getting my first paycheck and getting so excited. I could finally afford what I had wanted for the longest time. It wasn't a video game. It wasn't a new soccer jersey. It was a solo soccer trainer, one of those balls with a rope attached to it that you wrap around your waist. I could play in the backyard for hours, never having to chase after another ball. This one investment allowed me to enhance my game so much. I started using every paycheck to purchase soccer equipment. I don't regret a single thing I bought, because it all has gotten me to where I am today.

80. Never fade from who you are.

Success changes people. It is hard to stay on the path to your dreams while you are getting hit from both sides to be someone or something different. Never let the victories get to your head. Never let the haters get to your heart. This journey that you are on is going to be a rollercoaster but you can't become someone you aren't. People start to focus on money or the fame. They start to care more about their stat sheet than their improvement. Stick to your morals. You will need to overcome a lot of peer pressure to stick to the ethics that you were raised with. Stay true to your heart.

Although you may receive the college scholarship you wanted or the professional contract, you aren't done yet. Don't think that you can now become a lazy superstar. Don't think that life is now just going to be handed to you because you conquered one of your goals. Keep fighting. Always think about that 4-year-old version of yourself and remember why they loved the game so much. Play for that kid. Keep that kid in your heart as you progress through your career. Never lose sight of who you truly are. Don't let anyone or anything change you.

Story: When I signed my first contract, I was completely ecstatic. I had finally conquered all of my dreams. I knew the sky was the limit but a part of me said, "Now what?" I didn't know what to do with all that money and all that attention. I let it get the best of me. It changed me as a person and I had forgotten every moral I had. I lost control of my life and my career took a hit. I had lost so much focus that soccer wasn't even my first priority anymore. My life was turned on its head. I knew I had to refresh my memory back to the younger version of myself. I had to remember how hard I fought to make my dreams a reality. I couldn't let all that work go to waste. I needed to be true to myself and keep pushing for greatness.

81. Find your niche.

Every soccer player has it. Whether it is a specific attribute or certain move on the field. Every player has that one skill that always stands out. What is yours? Discover yourself as a soccer player and figure out why coaches love you the most. Ask your coaches and your teammates. Watch footage of your games. Is it your speed? Is it your shooting ability or your physicality? If you don't have one, create one. Give yourself a niche that will set you apart from the rest of the players.

Once you find that trait, make it explode. Work on it every day and keep improving it.

Some soccer players focus only on their weaknesses and don't worry about making their strengths better. They spend everyday trying to improve their weak spots; all while their strengths are slowly getting worse. Those types of players end up being nothing but average. Don't be an average player. Find your niche and train it as much as you can. Obviously, still work to improve your weaknesses, but don't neglect the niche. It is necessary to be able to catch a coach's attention. Your niche will catch the coach's eye, and the rest of your skillsets will make him or her love you.

Story: Speed has always been my niche. As a youth player, I would stay after practice and do speed training. I brought my speed parachute to practice and would do 50 or so sprints after the training session ended. My teammates wondered why I worked on my speed when I was already the fastest player on the team. I told them the reason why I was the fastest player on the team was because I worked on my speed training consistently. I wasn't going to let any of them catch me, ever. Just because you are good at something doesn't mean you can't get better. No one can touch your go-to skill. My teammates thought I was crazy. I thought I was determined. And my future told me I was right.

82. Don't let your emotions get to you.

Defenders will spit in your face. Referees will miss calls. Coaches will sub you out. Fans will antagonize you. The ball won't always bounce in your favor. But how do you respond when these things happen? Every soccer player gets emotional at times. They either get too excited, or too angry. They get too nervous, or too anxious. Don't let your emotions overwhelm you. Whenever your mind starts to get in the way of your playing, snap back to the big picture. Don't let little moments in games ruin the whole game for you. Bad things happen, but how you respond can determine the outcome of the game and your career.

A coach or scout will immediately stop being interested in you if they see you lose your head. Who cares if the opponent pushes you when you don't even have the ball? Who cares if a referee disallows one of your goals for offside? Let it go and count your blessings. You are too good to let the little things get you off your game. Always control your emotions. Scouts will watch you play in championships and in practices. No matter the circumstance, you need to be able to keep your cool when things get heated. Stay on their radar by controlling your emotions.

Story: I let my emotions get the best of me once in high school and I will never forget it. We were playing our rivals and one of the defenders kept pushing me and tripping me when the ball was on the other side of the field. I was getting so angry but I tried to stay focused. Then, I got the ball and fired a shot into the back of the net. I celebrated by running directly to the defender and spreading my arms right in front of him as I stared into his eyes. I taunted him and received a yellow card. My coach refused to put me back in the game, because he feared me losing control of my emotions again. I could have scored another 4 or 5 goals that game. I was so angry, but the only person I could be angry at was myself. Stay calm and stay focused.

83. Embrace the obstacles.

Becoming a professional soccer player is not easy. Don't expect to reach your dreams on a nice and easy ride through the journey. You will get beaten. You will get injured. You will be told that you'll never make it. Embrace those moments, because they are getting you ready for the big time. Every obstacle can be a lesson. And every obstacle WILL make you stronger. The saying "What doesn't kill you makes you stronger" is 100% true. Don't shy away from obstacles in your life. Don't look for the easy way out. Push through the obstacles and you will become better for it.

I guarantee that there are so many players out there who could've gone pro, but didn't, because of some stupid setback they faced. They could have easily stuck to the goal and pushed through it. But not everyone is strong enough to reach the highest of levels. Don't fail yourself. Take obstacles head on. Embrace the defeats. Accept that not everything is going to end in your favor. You will get rejected, and you will fail. Keep your head up and keep your eyes on the prize. If becoming a professional soccer player were easy, everyone would be doing it.

Story: I had a tryout for a professional team in the top division of Holland. I was so pumped. I worked my ass off and scored plenty of goals at practice. I was so sure that I was going to get offered a contract. At the end of the tryout the coach pulled me into his office and told me that I wasn't experienced enough to make it with his club. I was devastated, but I didn't give up. A lot of people give up at the first sign of failure. If I would have gone home and chosen a different career, I never would have reached my dreams of playing professional soccer. But I embraced this obstacle. I went home and trained harder. I got the experience I needed to make it as a pro. We need experiences like those to make us mentally stronger. We need obstacles in our lives.

84. Promote your victories.

Victories will be plentiful on your journey to success. Don't rub them in people's faces. Don't make people feel bad because they aren't as good as you. But at the same time, promote those victories. Don't be shy to let the world know just how good you are. Post on Facebook how your team just won a big tournament. Post a picture on Instagram with you holding that big trophy. Create a Snapchat story of you completing hard training drills. Make yourself be heard, seen, and appreciated. The people that don't understand you will think you are cocky. But the people that matter will be impressed. Promoting your successes and accomplishments make people aware of just how good you are. When people think you are good, your opportunities will grow.

Promote yourself beyond the Internet as well. Talk to people about your accomplishments. Tell those stories of you scoring 5 goals and beating your rivals in the conference championship. Impress people who have never even seen you play a single soccer game. How are people going to know how good you are if you never bring it up? Make it known that you will one day become a professional soccer player and people will help you get there. People want to be a part of success, no matter whose it is. Promote everything you do. Make yourself a big deal.

Story: I once posted a video of myself shooting a soccer ball from distance into a garbage can. I didn't think it was a big deal at the time. Little did I know, people were watching. I got a message from the general manager of my former team and he had seen the video. He wasn't sure if I was still playing after I had injured my knee. Once he saw the video, he immediately knew I had been training and he wanted me back in Europe. A simple video that I posted on Facebook was noticed all the way in another continent and it led to my comeback from a horrific injury. Now, I love posting videos of myself training or scoring goals. You can never underestimate the outreach of promoting yourself.

85. Train/play overseas at least once.

Playing in the same continent your whole life will make your game very 1-dimensional. There are so many different styles of soccer in the world. You may think that here is only one way to play soccer, but you are very wrong. If you don't believe me, try it out. I dare you. You won't become the best possible soccer player by staying in one place with the same competition your whole life. Expand your horizons. Playing in Europe, or Latin America, or even Africa can help you improve your game to new heights. Even if it is just for a couple training sessions, you will learn so much about how the game is played. Your game will slowly start to evolve.

Don't be scared or hesitant. Just go. Go right now and buy the ticket to England, or Germany, or Brazil. There will always be teams that will accept an extra player for training sessions. Make the investment in yourself. If you can't afford it, do some fundraising. Your soccer dreams shouldn't be taken lightly. Fundraising sucks, but it will be worth it. I wouldn't be putting this advice in this book if I didn't think it would benefit you. Head to a different country and I guarantee you will discover a different meaning to the word "soccer." Expand your horizons and your game will improve.

Story: The first time I left the country was for soccer. I went to Spain, and I didn't expect the game to be much different from what I had seen in America. I couldn't have been more mistaken. The pace of the game in Spain was so much quicker. They focused so much on the precision of passes and how they approached dribbling. I remember feeling like we weren't even playing soccer anymore. It was like they were playing their own sport. That experience really opened my eyes and I fell in love with the European style of play. Staying in the same place can lead to a 1-dimensionsal style. Take the risk and leave the country. Discover the world.

86. Play with players older than you.

Playing against people your own age will not improve your game to the point where it needs to be, especially if you are the best one on the team. Put yourself in playing scenarios where you are surrounded by bigger, stronger, and better opponents. The best way to do this is to play with squads that are older than you. If you have an older sibling, take advantage of it. Train with them. When you train with people that push you to your limits, you will improve greatly. Older players have more experience, and they usually have more skills. Playing against them will improve all assets of your game. Watching them will help you learn. Don't shy away from challenging them. Have the confidence to treat them as your equal.

Once you start playing or training with older players, then playing with people your own age will be almost too simple. You are too good to be playing with people your own age. Try out for older teams and surround yourself with people who are beyond what you are used to. The game only gets quicker and more physical as you grow up. Why not get used to that style now? Know that you are good enough to play with the big boys. Always seek opportunities to train with older players.

Story: Right before I got into high school, I went to Memphis to play a soccer tournament with a team that was 3 years older than me. I was so nervous. All of these guys were twice my height. I would get hit or pushed to the ground every time I tried to dribble the ball. I quickly learned that I couldn't hold onto the ball for too long. I got the ball and I got rid of it right away. My game had to be quick or I would get knocked on my ass. When I returned home from that tournament, my game was so much quicker than everyone else on my normal team. Training sessions seemed to be in slow motion because I was used to playing with the older guys. I learned so much from just one tournament and my game improved greatly.

87. Don't get burned out.

It is easy to get burned out when all you do is soccer, soccer, and more soccer 24/7. If you feel that you need a breather, don't hesitate. Take a break. Don't drive yourself crazy. Especially if you are pushing yourself as much as you should be, then you deserve a second to keep your sanity. Soccer can be exhausting mentally, physically, and emotionally. So many players end their careers early because they lose their passion or drive. They have just had enough of dedicating their lives to soccer. I would rather see you take a break for a couple days and come back refreshed, than just end your dreams altogether because you couldn't handle the lifestyle.

Pride is the key to not getting burned out. Be proud of what you have done and what you are still to do. It is okay to be exhausted. It is okay to need a break every once in a while. Just know that your dreams are always in sight as long as you never give up. Soccer is a beautiful sport. It is the best sport in the world. When you feel like you are getting burned out, just remember the sound of the ball hitting the back of the net. Remember the smell of the fresh cut grass. Remember the feeling of winning championships. It will all be worth it in the end. Take a break, but come back harder than ever. Your dreams are waiting.

Story: I have never gotten even close to getting burned out, but I know a lot of players that have and just gave up. Players give up because the sport gets too hard and too demanding. I understood at an early age that if I wanted to become a professional soccer player, I needed to be committed. I needed to be willing to make sacrifices that the average kid doesn't have to make. It isn't easy, but I promise you it is worth it. I don't get how someone could get halfway, and then give up on a dream that brings so much happiness. I take breaks every now and then, but I could never walk away from such a beautiful game. Soccer is my joy.

88. Stretch!

Stretching should not be taken lightly. Flexibility is the key to a healthy career. You can't become a professional soccer player if you aren't healthy. Coaches aren't going to want to sign a player with hamstring problems. Stretch when you wake up. Stretch before games. Stretch after games. Stretch before you go to bed. Stretching should consistently be in your daily routine. Stretching will keep you on the soccer field. It will help your muscles be in top form for whatever moves you make. Don't be injury-prone. You could even sign up for a yoga class. Watch YouTube videos of how to properly stretch before and after training sessions. Find out which of your muscles are tight. Physical therapists are able to analyze your whole body and tell you what needs work. Invest the time and money into aligning your body and getting healthy. Your career will thank you.

Stretching also falls into the category of "warming up for games." Coaches are watching you. They can tell if you are injury-prone just by how seriously you take stretching before games. They keep an eye out for flexible players, because those are the ones that rarely get injured. Challenge yourself to do the splits. Challenge yourself to kick above your head. Flexibility can lead to opportunities when you are in front of the goal and the ball is coming at a difficult angle or height. Range of motion will make it easier to score, to win tackles, and to gain every inch possible.

Story: Lack of stretching kept me from signing my first contract when I was 18-years-old. I pulled my hamstring when I was on trial in Sweden. The team was ready to offer me a contract, but I wouldn't have been able to play the rest of the season because of the injury. I had to go back home and attend college for a year before going back and trying again. Stretching would have added another whole year onto my professional career, at least. Take it seriously.

89. Relax.

There is no place for panicking on the soccer field. You need to be elegant and precise at all times, with or without the ball. It is easy to tell when a player is confident on the ball or not. Confident players are more laid back and don't stress under high pressure. Players lacking confidence get choppy with their touches and keep their heads down when under pressure. Be that relaxed player that doesn't worry, even when you are surrounded by 4 defenders and you're stuck in the corner. There is always a way out, so don't panic. Take a deep breath and analyze the situation. You aren't going to find the best option by panicking and losing the ball.

Scouts look for players who embrace pressure and don't let it get the best of them. They love players who are relaxed in any and every situation. You will never be put in a situation where you can't come out victorious. Always remember that in the back of your mind. Soccer is a fast sport. You can't panic your way to achieving your dreams. Life is good, and you are good at life. The same thing goes for soccer. Stay calm.

Story: When I am under pressure, I start picturing shapes. Not only does it bring me back to a happy time in my childhood daycare school, but it also helps me figure out the best solutions for getting out of the pressure. When I have the ball in the corner of the field and 2 defenders are closing down on me, I picture triangles and rectangles where I could play the ball to escape the pressure. I look at the triangles between the players' legs. I look at the rectangles to either side of them. I even look over them to see if I have enough room to play a ball in the air. I stay calm, because no pressure is unbreakable. There is always an escape route. I am confident enough in my abilities to play the ball through those shapes that I have pictured in my mind. Panicking is for scared players. The fearless always prosper.

90. Put your body on the line.

Risk everything, especially in the deciding moments of a match. If the ball is at a standstill on the goal line, you better be throwing all of your weight at that ball. I don't care if you go headfirst; push that ball over the goal line. Be willing to get bruised and beaten. Be willing to spill some blood. The truly successful players don't think twice about putting their body on the line when times call for it. Soccer is a game of inches and small victories. Any small victory could be the key factor towards a big victory. Fight for every tackle. Fight for every header. Scouts want fighters. They want players who are willing to risk injury for reward. There are too many weak and scared players in the world. Fear nothing and fight for everything.

This approach should be taken off the field toward your dreams as well. Dreams aren't easy, especially the one that you have chosen. Put your body on the line at all times. You can never be hesitant when it comes to fighting for your dreams. You have to make split second decisions to go all-in or nothing at all. Go all out, every day, all day. Put yourself through workouts that shouldn't be humanly possible. Sign up for karate lessons. Play pick-up football games. Train your body to take a beating. The beatings you endure will never be enough to knock you down. Put your body on the line for your dreams. They deserve it.

Story: When I first tore my ACL, I didn't even know that it was torn at first. I thought I just twisted it and the burning sensation would go away. We only had one game left in the season and we needed a point to avoid relegation. I definitely shouldn't have played, but I knew I needed to. I strapped on a huge knee brace and took the field. I ended up scoring 2 goals in a 3-3 draw that saved us from relegation. This single game built up my reputation as one of the toughest players in the league. I put my body on the line because my team needed me. Players who don't hesitate to risk everything are the ones who can achieve anything.

91. Know that someone is watching.

This advice doesn't just work because it adjusts your mentality. It works because it is usually true. There is always someone watching. Even when you are alone, you need to consider yourself as a fan. You can't tell me you don't gain a little bit of confidence in yourself when you hit an upper-90 shot, even when you are alone. Your opinion matters more than anyone's. But when you aren't alone, treat every set of eyes as an opportunity to advance your career. The world is smaller than you think and you never know when a bystander will say, "You have to check out this player that I watched." People are watching your skills. Always shoot for impressing everyone around you on the field. Be worth their time to stop and observe.

It is important to act like someone is always watching, but this shouldn't only improve your technical skills. The little things you do should be affected as well. Act like a professional at all times. Carry yourself properly. Have positive body language. Prove that you are a class act. Your every move is being judged at all times, on and off the field. People pay attention to the little things. Teachers see you walking down the halls. Coaches see you hanging out with your friends before games. Always be on top of your game. You don't want people to get a bad impression of you.

Story: When I was playing at a showcase in high school, our team was struggling. We were down at halftime to a team that we should have been beating. I walked off the field disappointed, with my head down and my hands in the air as if to ask, "What is wrong with you guys?" My coach ran over to me and said, "You see that coach walking away over there. He is a division-1 college coach. The last thing he saw was you complaining and moping around. You better straighten your act." I knew I messed up. I learned to always be positive and control myself. There are always eyes on you. Be careful.

92. Coach younger players.

Coaching the game opens your eyes and adds new dimensions to your understanding of the game. Soccer is a very complex sport. There is always knowledge out there to be learned. If you take the time to coach younger players, you will start to learn as well. You start to notice new things about the game that you've been playing your whole life. There will be lessons that you teach kids that you too could use to improve your own game. Younger players are always intrigued to learn, and that is always a trait that you need to hold onto. Always be willing to learn. Teaching them will help them grow as players. But you may be the one that learns more than they do.

Approaching the game as a player and approaching it as a coach are completely different. Good coaches understand the strategies and plans to bring a team together to play fluently. Good players can execute and put the coach's plans into action. But those people who are good at both coaching and playing are the ones who are extraordinary on the field. They see things that average players don't see. Always seek coaching positions or opportunities.

Story: I have coached younger players most of my life. Even when I was in middle school, my teammates would ask me questions and try to use me to expand their knowledge. When I got to an age where I could actually coach youth players, I started realizing how simple the game really is. It may be made up of a lot of complex ideas, but watching it from the sideline opened up a whole new point-of-view for me. I think I grew as much in one year of coaching as I did in 3 years playing. Younger players ask questions that really get you thinking. Coaching doesn't seem like it will help you as a player, but intellect is a huge key to success. I am so glad I decided to start coaching at a young age. Start now!

93. Pick an agent you can trust.

This advice won't come until you are ready to take that final step towards becoming a professional soccer player. However, I feel that this advice needs to be heard now, even as a teenager. Picking an agent doesn't just pertain to a sports agent, but also anyone that may represent you out in public. People that represent you are anyone that you associate yourself with. Don't bring people into your life if you don't think they represent you well. Bring yourself close to friends and family that you know understand you and love you. Trust them to the point where you can send them to a college coach and know they are going to help your case. Good people are rare, and the right good people are even harder to come by. Surround yourself with people who represent what you stand for.

When it comes to hiring an actual sports agent, be very cautious. There are agents out there who just want your money and don't care about your professional career. Only hire an agent who agrees to a percentage of your earnings, not a fee up front. Hire an agent who you would trust with your life, because essentially that is what you are putting in their hands. Your career's success depends on them.

Story: Starting to seek a professional career, I had an agent approach me wanting to represent me. I didn't know any better. I thought it was cool just to have an agent at all. So he charged an up front fee of a couple thousand dollars. He analyzed my skills and demanded video of my playing ability. In the end, that was pretty much the only interaction I had with the guy. I never heard from him again and I definitely didn't get any tryouts from the experience. From that point forward, I never trusted another agent again. I acted independently as my own agent. But I do believe that there are some good agents out there. Just make sure you take the time to find the right one. An agent can make or break your career.

94. Set up as many tryouts as possible.

Once you get an agent, have them set up as many tryouts as possible for you. Tell them you don't care about the level and you don't care about the location. Just tell them you want as many opportunities as possible. Your life-long dream is right in front of you. Don't let it get away. Now is the time to seek every chance you can get. Remember that all you need is a start for your professional career to begin and take off. Don't worry about starting off playing for the best team in the world, but obviously don't turn down a tryout if you get offered. Every tryout will either end with a contract offer or a lesson learned. Both of these things are positives. Therefore, every tryout will benefit your career in one way or another.

These tryouts may not always be what you are looking for, but you won't know until you try. You may tryout for one team as a center midfielder and realize you can't keep up in the center. You may find out you don't like the country of Germany when you are on trial there. You will slowly start to narrow down what your ideal location, position, pay, and atmosphere you want to start your career off with. Enjoy the journey.

Story: I had at least 10 tryouts before I signed my first professional contract. I got turned down time and time again. I wasn't smart enough. I wasn't fast enough. I wasn't talented enough. I heard it all. But I also slowly started to realize what kind of team I wanted to play for. I wasn't paying attention to their preferences. I knew I was good enough to play professionally. I was paying attention to where I wanted to start my career. I fell in love with the country of Sweden and I knew I wanted to make a life there. When the right opportunity came along, I took full advantage of it. I became a professional soccer player and my career was just taking off.

95. Don't chase the money.

Greed can be good, but it can also lead to discontent. The professional lifestyle is worth fighting for on its own. The money is a bonus, but don't let it control you. Chasing money doesn't lead to success. Chasing improvement is what leads you to the ultimate success. Money should never affect who you are as a person and who you are as a player. Happiness should be your main focus when you are living your life to the fullest. Players who chase money are the ones with short-lived careers because over time they just stop trying. They start worrying more about the size of their contracts than their abilities on the field.

Always remember where you started. The younger version of you never cared about the money. They played for fun. They probably didn't even know what money was when they started playing. Soccer has always been about having a good time. Don't let that change. You have gotten this far without millions of dollars in your pockets so don't let that slow you down. The less you focus on money, the more successful your career will get. It is always okay to negotiate for more money when talking about your contract, but never let it change your passion. Be passionate about soccer, not money.

Story: As I said earlier, I lost control of my life after I signed my first contract. I had so much money and I didn't know what to do with it. I cared more about the clothes I was buying than how I was performing on the field. Then I read a quote from Mia Hamm: "Somewhere behind the athlete you've become and the hours of practice and the coaches who have pushed you is a little girl who fell in love with the game and never looked back... play for her." This quote taught me to put aside all of the money, fame, and every other irrelevant part of life. I learned to focus on my love for the game. Display your passion and the money will come. Don't worry

96. Learn to be uncomfortable.

You will never improve if you live your whole life in constant comfort. Put yourself through hell. Think outside of the box. Live outside of society's boundaries. Talk to people who doubt you. Put yourself in scenarios where you don't feel comfortable. Play positions on the field that you don't usually play. Putting yourself in these types of spots will lead to your growth as a person and as a player. You need to train your mind and body to be comfortable at all times. Slowly become comfortable where you would normally be uncomfortable.

Placing yourself in the hands of distress will not be a fun experience. You will hate every second of it. But as you grow up, you will slowly start to realize that success isn't meant to be comfortable. Success is a constant fight for improvement. It is a lifestyle of consistently being placed in new scenarios. Professional soccer player seems like the perfect dream job, but you better be prepared to go through hell and back to make it a reality. Your body will hate you at times. You will be sore. Your mind will be exhausted. Your bones will feel weak. You will be in a constant stage of discomfort for 90% of your journey. If you don't learn to be uncomfortable, then your dreams will never come true. Enjoy the discomfort, because discomfort means growth.

Story: I was very socially awkward growing up. I never talked to anyone through middle school. I watched my favorite soccer players being interviewed and the thought of being interviewed terrified me. Then, I got to high school and was interviewed after every game. I hated it, but I learned to be in those uncomfortable situations. I learned to go beyond my fears and become well spoken. Now, I love interviews. I love talking to people and getting my face put in the newspaper.

97. Live and die for your team.

Team players are players who live and die for their team, no matter what kind of relationships they have with their teammates. If you truly want to be a team player, you have to seek opportunities to help your teammates grow. You have to take their improvement just as seriously as your own. Your teammates are a representation of you. Therefore, their success is your success. Being part of a good team will grow your number of opportunities in the future. Scouts aren't as interested when you are an amazing player but you can't help your team win a single soccer match. Always act as a teacher or coach for your teammates to turn to. It is your job to make sure they grow.

On top of their abilities, you also need to fight for their well-being. You need to protect them and make sure they trust you. Even off the field, you need to have the mentality that you would take a bullet for them. Coaches look for pit bulls on the field. They look for leaders that pick their teammates off the ground and pat them on the back. They look for leaders who critique their teammates performance to help them improve in the future. Treat your teammates like family. Fight for the logo on the front of the jersey instead of the name on the back. You should be the biggest fan of your own team. Carry that team crest on your heart everywhere you go.

Story: I make it clear to the world that no matter who I played for and no matter how good my team is, I always keep my team in my heart. When I score a goal, I kiss the logo. When we lose a game, I defend my teammates and take the blame. When my teammates are going through a rough patch, I pick them up and tell them how to improve. My team is my life and I would die for my coach, my teammates, my general manager, my board members, and even the facility janitors. If you carry that mentality, your team will be better for it. A successful team leads to a successful you.

98. Always keep your family close.

Always remember your roots. Remember where you came from. You should never lack motivation, because you have a whole family that is cheering you on and rooting for your success. When you always keep your family in your heart, you always have something to fight for. The success that you achieve in life will always be owed to your family. Your parents signed you up for soccer as a kid. They put a ball at your feet. They taught you tough life lessons. If you have any siblings, I guarantee they pushed you around and prepared you for the world. Your family deserves for you to reach your wildest of dreams. Whether you believe it or not, they are a huge reason as to why you are able to chase such a crazy dream. Be grateful.

Even if you don't have the best relationship with your family, always keep them in mind. Always use them as motivation to get you closer to your dream. Your mother gave birth to a wonderful child and raised you right. The teammates, coaches, and every other person you come across in life can and will influence you on your way to your dreams. But if you lose connection to your roots, then you will lose part of who you are. When you become successful, pay it back. Buy your mom a house. Buy your dad a nice car. Pay them back for everything they have done for you. If that isn't motivation in itself to become a successful pro soccer player, then I don't know what is.

Story: Before every match, I think about my family. Even if they are thousands of miles away, they are still my biggest fans. I know they want my success even more than I do. They are my motivation to score goals, to win, and to be as successful as possible. I could never repay my family for what they have done for me, but I can sure as hell fight to be the best version of myself to represent how amazing my family is. My parents deserve a child who dreams big and accomplishes it all, and so do yours.

99. Remember you are owed nothing.

Nothing in this life is going to be handed to you. You may have had a rich upbringing. You may have grown up in a big house and were the star of your high school. Those things don't mean that life is going to be easy, especially on the soccer field. Professional soccer players come from all different types of backgrounds. Some were spoiled and some had nothing. But what they all have in common is that they had to fight their whole lives to get to where they are now. You aren't born with the skills necessary to play professional soccer. You need to spend every second from the day you take your first steps until the day you die improving your skills and building your assets.

Having the mentality that the world owes you anything will make for a frightening reality check one day. You need to approach every day with the attitude that you need to earn your place in this world. Life is a privilege, but setting a goal of playing professional soccer was a choice. Earn every day and live like it can be taken away from you in a single second.

Story: I had a very privileged childhood. My parents were successful. I lived in a big house in a quiet suburb neighborhood. My parents gave me everything. When I started playing soccer, I quickly realized that nothing would come easy as it has in my childhood. People were knocking me down. Coaches were telling me how to do things. Those types of things only get worse and worse as you move through your soccer career. You can never wake up in the morning and feel like you deserve something from the world. You have to earn it. There is a reason it is called "chasing dreams" instead of "receiving your dreams." It isn't going to be handed to you. You deserve nothing until you earn it.

100. Put down this book and go!

Just because you read this book does not mean that you are automatically going to become a professional soccer player. This book just gave you the knowledge. Now you need to put that knowledge into action. Every soccer player in the world has access to this book, so now it is up to you to make yourself better than all of the rest. You have chosen a very difficult dream to chase in becoming a professional soccer player. Your dream will not come easily and the journey will be long and excruciating. Be patient and stay focused. You can do anything you put your mind to.

Now put down this book and go accomplish your dream of becoming a professional soccer player. Follow all 100 pieces of advice in this book and you will soon be playing in front of thousands of screaming fans, getting paid thousands or even millions of dollars, and playing the beautiful sport you love for a living. The time is yours.

Story: I wrote this book to tell teenagers what I wish I would have known at their age. I was able to accomplish my dreams without knowing all of this information at a young age, so I hope one day you are even more successful than I am. I have played many years of professional soccer now and I wouldn't want it any other way. You can do anything you put your mind to. Stay strong and stay committed. Your dreams are waiting to be conquered. Good luck and enjoy the ride.

Made in the USA
Middletown, DE
26 January 2020